poultry

the
hundred
menu
chicken
cookbook

the hundred menu chicken cookbook

by robert ackart

Illustrations by
Marjorie Zaum K.

Published in Association
with *Parade Magazine*

GROSSET & DUNLAP
A National General Company
Publishers   *New York*

For Carolyn, Dorothy, and Anne.

CONTENTS

FOREWORD

This book offers over one hundred recipes for chicken dishes from twenty-odd countries. For the most part, each is cooked and served in a single utensil. Menu ideas for a simple but complete meal are suggested at the end of each recipe for chicken *en casserole:* a hearty dish to accompany the casserole (rice, barley, bulgur, noodles, spaghetti, etc., and a few homemade breads), ideas for several kinds of salad, a guide to forty-one cheeses from eight countries (all readily available at supermarket or cheese shop), and some notions about fruit as dessert.

In addition to the one-pot chicken recipes, suggestions are offered for roasting chicken and for several different dressings to accompany it; for dishes made with chicken livers; and for various kinds of dumplings which may be served, if desired, as part of a casserole dish. The section on roasting chicken is included because of a personal prejudice; I thoroughly enjoy roast chicken, but often find its stuffing tasteless or soggy or both. My hope is to make suggestions which will avoid this pitfall.

The casserole recipes have been chosen for their variety; some are familiar, others exotic; some are light, others substantial; some are elegant party fare, others plain victuals. Regardless of their nationality or particular quality, they have all been adapted and tested for one of two techniques of preparation: 1) the chicken, dredged in seasoned flour, is browned, thus making its own sauce base or 2) the chicken is browned, removed from the cooking utensil, the components and sauce of the dish prepared, and the chicken replaced. I prefer the second method, but sometimes the first is either essential to the recipe or more convenient for the cook. In any case, the book is based upon mastery of only two cooking techniques.

Three considerations led to writing this book. One, the cost of chicken compared to that of other meats makes it attractive to homemaker and host, alike. Two, the varied national and geographical origins of these dishes permit their frequent use without danger of repeating flavors. And, three, the recipes, all of which "hold" well, require neither great time nor effort (½ hour to prepare them and about 1 hour to cook them); all have been adapted to readily available ingredients.

In preparing the casserole dishes, I recommend a 5-, 5½- or 6-quart casserole of enamelized iron. It is flame- and oven-proof, cleans easily, is attractive as a serving dish, and sufficiently large that the entire recipe may be prepared in the single utensil.

Unless otherwise stated, all recipes for the suggested menus serve six persons. If desired, they may be halved or doubled. Unless otherwise stated, they may also be refrigerated or frozen.

Last, the writing of a cookery book is almost as personal as the writing of one's memoirs; we put down what we have enjoyed and what we want to share. For this reason, I begin certain of these recipes with recollections of their sources in hope that these thumbnail sketches will whet your interest and enthusiasm.

Robert Ackart

Katonah, New York
1971

the
hundred
menu
chicken
cookbook

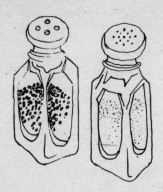

1. TO PLAN YOUR MEAL...

In this book, a typical menu reads:

Chicken with paprika
Noodles (p. 116)
Mixed green salad (p. 129)

Cheese and fruit, two items integral to every menu, are left to the choice of the cook. Chapter 6 cross-lists alphabetically and by nationality over forty cheeses, characterizes them, and suggests their availability.

Finding suitable fresh fruit in the supermarket is not always easy; it is usually delivered green, and for this reason must be bought two or three days before use and allowed to ripen. This should be done in a dry, shaded area, where the fruits do not touch each other. Thus, one is most often able to offer fresh fruit to end the meal. (A good, garden-variety apple, eaten with a complementary cheese, is among the best of "gourmet" treats!) Depending on how substantial the main dish is, you may want to dispense with fruit and conclude the meal with salad and cheese.

Experiment with menu-making for your own pleasure. The suggestions given here may act as guidelines, but they are just that—suggestive ideas—and not to be considered rigid. They may be altered to offer a national or regional meal (American or French or Middle Eastern, for example) or to offer what appeals as simply a pleasant combination of foods.

Alone in the kitchen, the cook is master artist, free to improvise, to explore, and, usually, to delight both family and friends. Indeed, I feel productions of the kitchen are supreme examples of creativity. The creation, it is true, disappears in very little time, but it gives intense, if transient, gratification to the eater.

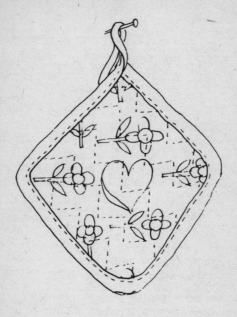

2. A LEXICON
FOR YOUR USE...

"Assemble and prepare all ingredients":   So often in the rush of present-day living we start a recipe without reading it. Suddenly we need an ingredient which we have not prepared or, worse, which we have neglected to buy. "Assemble and prepare all ingredients" begins each main-dish recipe as a reminder that cooking is easier and the results more satisfying if everything, ingredients and utensils, is ready and at hand.

"At this point you may stop and continue later":   is a signal useful to the cook unable to complete the dish at one time; also helpful if the cook prefers not to reheat the completed casserole. It is assumed that no more than 3 hours intervene in the preparation process; if so, the casserole should be refrigerated. Refrigerating will increase cooking time.

Bacon: (see *Salt pork*)

"Brown chicken; season":   Most of the recipes call for browning unfloured chicken; some, however, are more easily made with or actually require use of seasoned flour. To brown chicken, place the skin side down, season the up side with salt and pepper; when the chicken is turned, the seasoning will cook into the meat. Browning chicken pieces is not a pleasurable pastime; it is boring and can be messy. Once browned, however, the pieces may be frozen until needed. Brown a large quantity of chicken and keep it frozen against the day when you

3

want to make some dish or other. Browning the chicken is not absolutely necessary to these recipes; but the added flavor derived from doing so is ample recompense for the trouble.

There is another, less arduous, way of browning chicken: arrange the pieces, skin side down, on a broiler rack, season the top side with salt and pepper, and proceed as if you were going to make broiled chicken, lightly parbroiling until the top side is only *barely* golden; turn the pieces and repeat. The chicken essence and fat which drip through, once chilled and separated, are excellent in stock (the essence) and for use in cooking (the fat). (see also *Seasoned flour*)

Bulgur (also spelled bulghur): is cracked buckwheat groats, used throughout the Middle East as often as rice, having both a more distinctive texture and flavor than white rice. Because it has more body, it tends to "hold" better for delayed serving and for freezing. Available at all specialty and Middle Eastern food stores and, sometimes, at the supermarket.

Butter: is called for in these recipes, but in cooking, margarine serves equally well. You will find that 2 tablespoons butter (or margarine) and 2 tablespoons oil will suffice for browning undredged chicken; the chicken itself makes some fat. In browning floured chicken you may want to add butter and oil as needed.

Casserole: One of the aims of this book is to enable preparation of the main dish in one utensil or sometimes two. For this reason, use a commodious casserole. Casserole sizes are sometimes difficult to judge; they come in several gradations of size: 5-, 5½-, and 6-quart sizes are available. I use a 5½-quart enamelized iron casserole; it is big enough to work in, but sufficiently compact to keep the dish "together." It is also easily cleaned. For doubling recipes you will need a larger casserole.

Chicken broth: In these recipes, a 10½-ounce can of chicken broth is often called for. I use it undiluted. Chicken bouillon cubes or powder may be used to make chicken broth. The thrifty cook will make his own: save all bones from chicken dishes, as well as bits of skin and fat which may have been cut from the serving-pieces before cooking. Put these in a soup kettle, together with 1 or 2 bay leaves, a generous pinch of marjoram, sage, and thyme, and salt and pepper (I also add a bit of sugar); add water to cover and simmer for about 3 hours. Strain broth through a colander, then strain through a fine sieve into a tall, narrow container (this shape aids in the removal of the fat—I use a 2-quart plastic refrigerator jar). Allow to cool, chill overnight, and remove the

fat. This fat, incidentally, works very well in place of butter and oil for browning chicken.

Chicken fat: Fat removed from homemade broth or reserved from previous chicken-browning is admirable for browning the next chicken. (see also *"Heat butter and oil . . ."*)

Chick-peas: also called *garbanzos* (Spanish) and *ceci* (Italian), are available in 20-ounce cans. In this book, three chicken recipes call for chick-peas. *Hommos* (p. 141), a Middle Eastern spread which substitutes nicely for cheese, also uses chick-peas as its principal ingredient.

Condiments for curries: are mango chutney, chopped sweet pickle, raisins, chopped hard-boiled egg, chopped scallions, peanuts, pineapple tidbits, shredded coconut, and thin-sliced banana, served in small side dishes.

Curry: Curry powders may be made of five spices or fifty, all dried and ground before being combined. Commercial curry may blend fifteen or twenty herbs and spices. One of the better commercial varieties is compounded of cumin, coriander, turmeric, fenugreek, cardamon, and red and black peppers. In certain of these recipes, the curry is made from individual spices and herbs, giving quite a different flavor from commercial curry powder.

Deglaze: A term applied to the addition of liquid, usually broth or wine, to the casserole after the chicken is browned. Over high heat, cook the liquid until it boils, stirring and scraping until the bits of chicken left from browning are free and can become part of the sauce.

Doubling: All recipes in this book may be doubled. Many of the casserole recipes have been tripled or quadrupled for serving large groups at buffet suppers. (Chicken is a good buffet offering; it is moderately priced and, if thoroughly cooked, requires only minor surgery to separate meat from bone—indeed, a fork is sufficient.)

Eggplant: is a fruit, not a vegetable. A staple of Middle Eastern and Italian cooking, it is sadly underrated by the average American cook, who dredges it in egg and crumbs and then fries it. The several recipes for eggplant given here will, I hope, convince the reader of the versatility and subtlety of this beautiful food. Unless the recipe suggests peeling the eggplant, do not; the skin cooks easily.

Freezing: Unless noted to the contrary, the casserole recipes in this book will freeze. All frozen dishes should be thawed to room tempera-

ture before being reheated. Dishes made with rice, however, do not always freeze so successfully; the rice tends to lose its texture. Brown rice and bulgur hold their graininess more readily than white rice (and, if desired, both may be substituted for white rice in these recipes). To store, line an oven-proof serving dish or casserole with foil, arrange the completed recipe in it, and freeze. When it is thoroughly frozen, remove the foil pack from the dish, wrap it again in foil, and return to freezer. To use, peel foil from the frozen block, place block in casserole, thaw to room temperature, and heat to serve.

Frozen foods: In general, I prefer using fresh foodstuffs rather than frozen products. Often, however, frozen foods are welcome time-savers. It is the consistency of frozen foods, once cooked, and not their taste, which I find disturbing. Frozen vegetables, for example, turn to mush if overcooked. Frozen chopped onion is difficult to cook until golden because of the high water content in it. Still, some of these recipes call specifically for frozen foods; when this occurs, use them in good faith.

Fruit, cooking with: The use of fruit in combination with meat is a contribution of the Middle East and Orient to world cuisine. A most felicitous gift, it is not generally practiced by Occidental cooks, but should be. The recipes here which call for various fruits—fresh, dried, or canned—are among my favorites.

Ginger (fresh):   Fresh ginger root is available at all Oriental and many specialty food stores. To keep it: buy a pound, peel off the bark, cut the root into walnut-sized pieces, put them in a jar, add dry sherry to cover, and store in the refrigerator. The root will keep indefinitely this way. I prefer the tang of fresh ginger to the milder taste of candied ginger; the latter, however, is available at supermarkets.

"Heat butter and oil . . .":   but not to the point that they smoke or discolor. A drop of water in the casserole, wildly dancing, will show that it is time to add the chicken for browning. The browning process seals in the juices and sears the flesh for extra flavor. Chicken fat may also be used, although it spatters more than a combination of butter (or margarine) and oil.

Herbs: Many flavor variations in this book derive from herbs. Whenever possible, use fresh ones; their taste is only remotely related to the taste of dried herbs. If you have a spare window sill, try growing a few. Basil, marjoram, parsley, sage, summer savory, and thyme are

obliging plants, eager to thrive and to flavor a dish. If you use dried herbs, select the best brand available; do not stint here, for quality makes the difference between real bouquet and very little taste of any kind.

Julienne: is a term derived from French cooking, meaning cut into very thin lengthwise slices or strips.

Margarine (see also *Butter*):   may be used in place of butter in these recipes; or you may use half and half. For delicate dishes—such as buttered rice or noodles—try unsalted butter, a delight to the palate.

Marinating: Do not hesitate to lengthen the suggested marinating times, but never shorten them. Marination tenderizes the chicken and adds its own particular flavor. I recommend marinating at room temperature. If the marination period is longer than four hours, allow four hours *outside* the refrigerator and the remaining time *inside.* Unless otherwise specified, save the marinade as an ingredient of the sauce.

Oil: In cooking, use either the finest grade of pure olive oil, a mixture of half olive and half corn oils, or a tasteless oil such as peanut or sesame seed. In salad dressing, the finest grade of pure olive oil is recommended; it will add flavor to the dressing without being heavy.

Oven cooking (see also *Top-of-stove cooking*):   While these recipes are all suggested for oven cooking at 350°F., covered, for 1 hour, you may, if preferred, cook the casseroles on top of the stove. This is easily done if your range is equipped with a "thermal eye" and temperature control; otherwise, a comfortable simmer and a watchful eye will do nicely.

Parsley: is available in two varieties (curly leafed and Italian flat leafed) and in three forms, fresh, dried, and frozen. Use fresh whenever possible. Rinse the parsley in cold water, shake off all excess water, put in a container with tight-fitting lid, and store in the refrigerator. Treated this way, parsley keeps well many days. Frozen parsley tends to be watery and I think dried parsley tastes like hay.

Pepper: There are three popular peppers: black, white, and red. Unless otherwise specified, black pepper is called for in these recipes (albeit white may also be used). I prefer to use peppercorns, grinding fresh pepper as I need it. White pepper does not differ from black; it has merely had the dark hull removed. Red pepper differs markedly

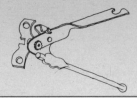

from both black and white and from its red-colored cousin, paprika; in these recipes it is *not* used unless specifically directed.

Preparation time: With few exceptions, the rule of this book is that any of the chicken casseroles may be made ready for cooking in 30 minutes; and cooked in about 1 hour. This timing assumes a certain expertise on the part of the cook; as you master the techniques of the book, you will gain speed. While the casserole is cooking, the remaining portions of the meal may be prepared (yeast breads are the only menu items requiring advance preparation).

Refrigerating: Just as the majority of casseroles may be frozen, so may they be refrigerated. This enables the cook to prepare the meal a day ahead, chill it, and reheat it before serving. Please note, however, that the most successful reheating is done after the chilled casserole has come fully to room temperature. Remove it from the refrigerator 2 or 3 hours before reheating and reheat gently to avoid overcooking. If a dish cannot be refrigerated, notation to that effect is made.

Salt pork: Rendering ¼ pound salt pork, diced, for use in browning chicken makes a richer casserole. Some of these recipes direct doing so; many may be so treated if desired. Recipes which offer a delicate or light flavor are better prepared as suggested. The pork bits, reserved and drained on absorbent paper, make a tasty garnish, cooked with the casserole or added at the time of serving. These comments on salt pork also apply to 4 strips of bacon, diced, and used in the same way.

Scalding: It is not necessary to boil milk to scald it (boiling often makes cleaning the pan difficult). Over high heat, cook the milk until its surface shimmers, then continue with the recipe as directed.

Seasoned flour: For 12 to 18 serving-pieces of chicken (see *"Serving-pieces of chicken for 6 persons"*), use ⅔ cup flour, 1½ teaspoons salt, and ½ teaspoons pepper, shaken together in a waxed paper bag, in which the chicken is then shaken, two or three pieces at a time. Add a bit of flour to casserole when making sauce. For seasoned flour, I prefer white pepper which will not speckle the sauce.

"Serving-pieces of chicken for 6 persons":   This phrase, (referring to young chicken—fryers or broilers, not stewing fowl) appears in each

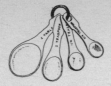

of the casserole recipes. Often chicken parts are available, so that you can choose what you like best. I prefer the second joint, or thigh; it is more flavorful and moist than other parts of chicken, and much less expensive than the "socially acceptable" breast, which can be dry, stringy, and flavorless. These recipes, however, may be prepared equally well with whole young chicken which you cut into serving-pieces. Depending upon the parts of the chicken used and their size, allow two or perhaps three pieces per serving.

Top-of-stove (range) cooking: These casseroles may be easily cooked on top of a stove equipped with a "thermal eye" and temperature control. Lacking this, simmer gently and keep a watchful eye on the contents of the casserole. Recommended, however, is the carefree oven method, suggested in each recipe.

Turmeric: This tropical herb has very little flavor of its own, but it is of invaluable help in coloring curry dishes and also dishes made with rice. Saffron will give color, too, but it is costly and highly flavorful; save saffron for occasions demanding it.

Wine (cooking and table):   Recipes requiring wine should be cooked in enamelized or crockery ware; otherwise, the wine will take on the metallic taste of the utensil. If "1 bottle of wine" is called for, the American (25.6 ounces), French (24 ounces) or the German (23 ounces) measure may be used. (These measures are averages.) Unless otherwise suggested, *dry* wine, both red and white, is called for. "Cooking wine" does not exist, despite the wide use of that phrase. There is only good and not-so-good wine. It is unnecessary to cook with wine of fine vintage or costly price. Your palate, however, will convince you that the quality of the dish reflects the quality of wine used in it.

As for table wine, I do not hold that "with chicken, white wine." The heartier casseroles in this book taste better if served with red wine. White wine is always acceptable, and *vin rosé* is many times welcome. As for your selection, that I must leave to you; availability and prices are so much a matter of geographical location. You will do well to engage the interest of your local wine merchant. I do not recommend imported over domestic wines; there are admirable wines in both groups. Good wine, modestly priced or costly, must be ferreted out.

3. "OUR MENU IS CHICKEN..."

Chicken with Apples

French

About a two-hour drive from Paris, in the hamlet of St. Maurice-sur-Aveyron, is an eighteenth-century hunting lodge, the home of Mme. Daisy Singer-Dugardin, where there is always warm hospitality, good talk, delicious food—and a jigsaw puzzle on the card table. Perhaps, next to my own home, this is the place I think of most often in terms of serene coziness. Although chicken with apples is a Norman dish, I first enjoyed it at Mme. Singer-Dugardin's "La Domerie."

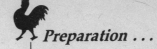

You will need ...	Preparation ...
	Assemble and prepare all ingredients.
2 Tbs butter 2 Tbs oil Serving-pieces of chicken for 6 persons Salt Pepper	In casserole, heat butter and oil and brown chicken; season.
⅓ cup cognac	In saucepan, warm cognac, ignite, and pour over chicken. Allow flame to burn out.
4 apples, peeled, cored, and sliced 2 onions, chopped	Add apples and onion.
1 cup apple cider 1 cup sour cream 1 Tbs flour 2 Tbs parsley, chopped 1 tsp tarragon ¾ tsp salt ¼ tsp pepper ½ tsp paprika	Combine cider, sour cream, flour, and seasonings; stir until smooth and pour over contents of casserole.
	At this point you may stop and continue later.

Cooking ...

Bake, covered, at 350° for 1 hour, or until chicken is tender.

If desired, 2 cups of cider (or apple juice) may be used; omit sour cream and use 2 Tbs flour. For flavor variations, omit tarragon and use ¼ tsp each cinnamon, clove, and nutmeg.

Serve with ... French Bread (p. 120)
Watercress Salad (p. 132)

Chicken with Artichoke Hearts

French

This recipe is stolen from Jack Kauflin, a friend living in California, who found the dish at a restaurant in Bordeaux and persuaded the chef to part with his directions for it. Thus, my thieving use of it, even with acknowledgment to Mr. Kauflin, is unpardonable; but the flavor of the casserole may, perhaps, stand as my excuse.

You will need ...	Preparation ...
	Assemble and prepare all ingredients.
¼ lb. salt pork, diced 18 small white onions, peeled	In casserole, render salt pork until crisp; remove to absorbent paper and reserve. Add onions to fat and glaze, stirring occasionally; remove and reserve.
Serving-pieces of chicken for 6 persons	Brown chicken and remove.
6 medium potatoes, peeled and diced 3 carrots, scraped and sliced thin	To remaining fat, add potatoes and carrots, stirring to coat well; remove. (A little additional butter may be added, if necessary.)
2 9-oz. packages frozen artichoke hearts ½ tsp salt ½ tsp pepper	In casserole, arrange chicken, then pork bits and onions, and finally potatoes and carrots. Top with layer of artichoke hearts. Season.
	At this point you may stop and continue later.

continued ...

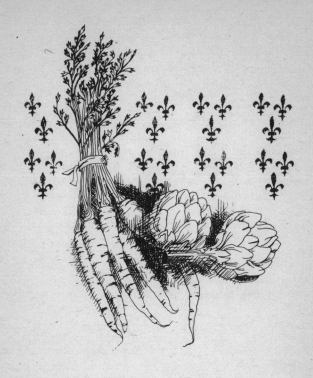

Cooking ...

1   **cup chicken broth, boiling**

Over contents of casserole, pour chicken broth; bake, covered, at 350° for 1 hour, or until chicken is tender.

Substitutes for chicken broth: ½ cup broth, ½ cup dry white wine; *or,* ½ cup water, ½ cup wine.

Serve with ... French Bread (p. 120)
Spinach Salad with mushrooms (p. 131)

Chicken with Avocado

American   (Does not refrigerate; Does not freeze)

A delicately flavored dish with an elegant appearance.

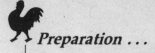

You will need ...	*Preparation ...*
	Assemble and prepare all ingredients.
2 **Tbs butter** 2 **Tbs oil** **Serving-pieces of chicken for 6 persons** **Salt** **Pepper**	In casserole, heat butter and oil and brown chicken; season. Remove.
6 **scallions, chopped (with as much green as possible)**	In remaining fat, sauté scallions.
3 **Tbs flour** ¼ **tsp cinnamon** ½ **tsp chili powder**	Stir in flour and blend; add spices and cook gently for a few minutes.
2 **cups orange juice** **Grated rind of 1 orange**	Add orange juice and rind and cook, stirring, until sauce thickens. Replace chicken. At this point you may stop and continue later.
	Cooking ...
	Bake, covered, at 350° for 1 hour, or until chicken is tender.
2 **ripe avocados, peeled and cut in lengthwise slices**	Over contents of casserole, arrange avocado slices in star shape; bake, uncovered, for 10 minutes.

Serve with ... Rolls (p. 121)
Cucumber Salad (p. 127)

Chicken with Bacon Sauce

American

This dish is pungent and hearty; appetizing for fall or winter meals.

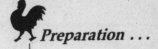

You will need ...

Preparation ...

Assemble and prepare all ingredients.

¼ lb. thick-sliced bacon, diced

In casserole, render bacon until crisp; remove to absorbent paper and reserve.

Seasoned flour
Serving-pieces of chicken for 6 persons

In seasoned flour, dredge chicken and brown in remaining fat.

1 bay leaf, broken
½ tsp thyme
1 tsp sage

Sprinkle with seasonings and any remaining flour.

At this point you may stop and continue later.

Cooking ...

2 cups chicken broth
1 cup light cream

Combine broth and cream and pour over contents of casserole. Bake, covered, at 350° for 1 hour, or until chicken is tender. When serving, garnish with reserved bacon.

Serve with ... New Potatoes (p. 117)
Salad of your choice

Chicken with Bananas

Mexican   (Does not freeze)

This dish, with its unusual blend of ingredients and flavors, elicits expressions of incredulity, surprise, and—best of all—pleasure.

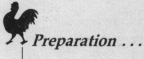

You will need ...	*Preparation ...*
	Assemble and prepare all ingredients.
Seasoned flour Serving-pieces of chicken for 6 persons 2 Tbs butter 2 Tbs oil	In seasoned flour, dredge chicken. In casserole, heat butter and oil and brown chicken. Remove.
2 onions, chopped 2 cloves garlic, chopped	In remaining fat, cook onion and garlic until translucent.
Juice from 1-lb. can whole Italian tomatoes Remaining seasoned flour	Combine juice with flour; blend until mixture is smooth and add to casserole.
3 carrots, sliced thin Reserved Italian tomatoes ½ tsp each: oregano, red pepper flakes (or to taste), thyme	Add carrots, tomatoes, and seasonings. Replace chicken. At this point you may stop and continue later.

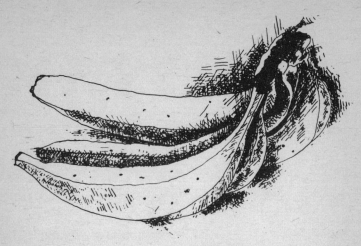

Cooking ...

1 cup chicken broth, boiling ½ cup dry white wine	Combine liquids and pour over contents of casserole; bake, covered, at 350° for 35 minutes.
12 to 18 pitted prunes	Add prunes and continue to cook, covered, for 20 minutes.

3 firm bananas, peeled,
    sliced lengthwise,
    and halved
	Add banana slices and continue to cook, covered, for another 15 minutes.

Serve with ... White Bread (p. 120)
or
Corn Muffins (p. 122)
Beans in Garlic oil (p. 127)

Chicken with Beans and Sausage

Algerian

This North African *cassoulet* is ideal for serving more than six persons; the present recipe, serving ten to twelve, may be halved for fewer people. A large casserole or two smaller ones is required.

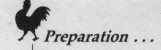

You will need ...

Preparation ...

Assemble and prepare all ingredients.

2 Tbs butter	In large casserole, heat butter and oil and brown chicken; season. Remove.
2 Tbs oil	
24 serving-pieces of chicken	
Salt	
Pepper	

6   links Italian sweet sausage
6   links Italian hot sausage

Cut sausage links into ¾" segments. In remaining fat, render them until crisp. Remove.

Discard all but 4 Tbs fat; spread this evenly over sides of casserole.

4   20-oz. cans white kidney beans, rinsed and drained

In casserole, arrange alternate layers of chicken and beans; top with sausage segments.

1   6-oz. can tomato paste
2   cups chicken broth
3   cloves garlic, pressed
1½ tsp salt
½ tsp pepper
2   tsp sugar

Blend together these six ingredients.

At this point you may stop and continue later.

Cooking ...

Over contents of casserole, pour liquid mixture. Bake, covered, at 300° for 1½ hours, or until liquid is absorbed. (The *cassoulet* should be moist and firm.)

Serve with ... Green Salad with White Grapes (p. 128)

Chicken with Beef

American

This recipe, a variant of Brunswick stew, traditionally prepared with squirrel, is very easily made. With a hot bread and salad, it constitutes a full and satisfying meal.

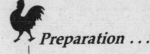

You will need ...	*Preparation ...*
	Assemble and prepare all ingredients.
1½ lbs. beef chuck, cut in bite-size pieces Water 1 Tbs salt ½ tsp pepper 1 tsp sugar 2 bay leaves	In casserole, combine meat and water just to cover; add seasonings. Bring to boil and simmer, covered, 1 hour.
Serving-pieces of chicken for 6 persons 1 20-oz. can tomatoes 1 1-lb. can cream-style corn 4 onions, chopped 1 9-oz. package frozen okra, cut in 1" sections ½ tsp celery seed	To contents of casserole, add chicken and remaining ingredients. At this point you may stop and continue later.

Cooking ...

	Bake, covered, at 350° for 45 minutes.
1 1-lb. can Irish potatoes, drained	Add potatoes and continue cooking for 15 minutes, or until chicken is tender.

Serve with ... Corn muffins (p. 122) *or*
Rolls (p. 121)
Mixed Green Salad (p. 129)

Chicken with Beer
Flemish

I found this dish at a modest restaurant on the rue des Bouchers, a picturesque street in Brussels known for its inexpensive eating places. Newly arrived from a wintry Germany, I made my way to one of these restaurants where I feasted on chicken with beer, bread—as only the Belgians and French can make it—and a hearty red wine. Any food-lover traveling in Belgium should avail himself of the solid pleasures of the rue des Bouchers. In the Flemish sections of Europe, beer is used as a cooking liquid, just as wines are used in more familiar cuisines.

You will need ...	Preparation ...
	Assemble and prepare all ingredients.
¼ lb. salt pork, diced	In casserole, render salt pork until crisp; remove to absorbent paper and reserve.
Serving-pieces of chicken for 6 persons	In fat, brown chicken and remove.
4 onions, sliced thin	In remaining fat, cook onions until translucent. Discard any excess fat.
2 Tbs flour ½ tsp each: marjoram, pepper, rosemary, thyme 1 tsp salt 1 tsp sugar 1 clove garlic, minced	Stir flour into onions. Add seasonings.
1 12-oz. can warm beer 2 Tbs cider vinegar	To contents of casserole, add beer; over high heat, cook, stirring constantly, until sauce thickens. Reduce heat; add vinegar and stir to blend mixture. Replace chicken and sprinkle pork bits over.
	At this point you may stop and continue later.

Cooking ...

Bake, covered, at 350° for 1 hour, or until chicken is tender.

Serve with ... Noodles (p. 116) *or*
Potato Pancakes (p. 117)
Salad of your choice

Chicken with Bing Cherries

French

A treatment of *poulet Montmorency* which can be prepared almost without effort *en casserole*.

You will need ...

Preparation ...

Assemble and prepare all ingredients.

2   Tbs butter
2   Tbs oil
    Serving-pieces of chicken for 6 persons
    Salt
    Pepper

In casserole, heat butter and oil and brown chicken; season. Remove.

1   cup port wine
    Syrup from 2 1-lb. cans pitted Bing Cherries
    Water, if needed
3   Tbs cornstarch

Combine liquids to equal 2½ cups. Add cornstarch, stirring until mixture is smooth. Add liquid to casserole and cook over high heat, stirring, until sauce thickens.

1   clove garlic, minced
    Rind and juice of 1 lemon
½   tsp powdered clove

Add seasonings and stir to blend mixture. Replace chicken.

At this point you may stop and continue later.

Cooking ...

Bake, covered, at 350° for 45 minutes; add reserved cherries and continue to cook for 15 minutes, or until chicken is tender.

Variation: Use seasoned flour to which are added ¾ tsp garlic powder and ¾ tsp paprika. In flour, dredge chicken and brown it. Combine 1 cup white wine, cherry syrup, and water as needed, to equal 2½ cups. Proceed as indicated above, omitting fresh garlic.

Serve with ... Brown Rice (p. 115)
Spinach Salad with mushrooms (p. 131)

Chicken with Bourbon

American

Perhaps this recipe is the American version of the French Chicken with Liqueur. Like its cousin from France, Chicken with Bourbon has a delicate flavor. The fact that it is made with whiskey is something of a conversation-maker.

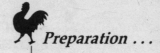

You will need ...	*Preparation ...*
	Assemble and prepare all ingredients.
Seasoned flour Serving-pieces of chicken for 6 persons 2 Tbs butter 2 Tbs oil	In seasoned flour, dredge chicken. In casserole, heat butter and oil and brown chicken.
½ cup bourbon whiskey	Warm whiskey, ignite it, and pour over chicken.
18 mushrooms, sliced 6 scallions, chopped	When whiskey flame disappears, add mushrooms and scallions; cook 5 minutes.
	At this point you may stop and continue later.

Cooking ...

1 cup light cream	Over contents of casserole, pour cream; bake, covered, at 350° for 1 hour, or until chicken is tender.
	If desired, ½ cup sour cream and ½ cup milk, combined, may be substituted for light cream; actually I prefer this.

Serve with ... Bulgur (p. 115)
Artichokes (p. 127)

Chicken with Brown Rice

American

When I was a child, we called this recipe "Ida's chicken." Ida came to our family when she was barely eighteen; I, too, was eighteen—eighteen months. Despite help from relatives, my mother needed assistance in caring for two infants ("I" was twins), a seven-year old son with a proclivity for breaking his arms, and a fourteen-year old daughter with a charming manner and a will of iron. Enter Ida! At once, she took over twins and kitchen and became in short time an expert "plain" cook. Ida's recipes were written in a school exercise book marked "Spelling —Richard" (the accident-prone brother mentioned above); her notations on my mother's directions usually consisted of listing ingredients she feared she would forget. Ingredients of which she was sure, amounts and methods have remained a mystery. This recipe complements Chicken with Bulgur (following), since both may be prepared with either brown rice or bulgur.

You will need ...

Serving-pieces of chicken
for 6 persons
½   lb. mushrooms, quartered
1   bay leaf, broken
1½ tsp salt
½   tsp pepper
1½ cups brown rice

3   cups chicken broth,
      boiling

Preparation ...

Assemble and prepare all ingredients.

In casserole, arrange chicken; add mushrooms in a layer. Mix seasonings and brown rice and add to casserole.

At this point, you may stop and continue later.

Cooking ...

Over contents of casserole, pour chicken broth; bake, covered, at 350° for 1 hour, or until chicken and rice are tender and liquid is absorbed.

Variation: Use white rice mixed with 1 minced garlic clove, a dash of cayenne, and either 1½ tsp turmeric *or* 1½ tsp curry powder *or* ½ tsp saffron.

Serve with ... Green Bean Salad with red onions (p. 128)

Chicken with Bulgur

Middle Eastern

For a dish so remarkably uncomplicated, this one boasts a fine subtlety of flavor.

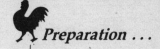

You will need ...

Preparation ...

Assemble and prepare all ingredients.

2	**Tbs butter**
2	**Tbs oil**
	Serving-pieces of chicken for 6 persons
	Salt
	Pepper

In casserole, heat butter and oil and brown chicken; season. Remove.

3	**onions, chopped**
1	**clove garlic, chopped**

In remaining fat, cook onion and garlic until translucent.

1½ **cups bulgur**

Add bulgur, stirring to glaze well.

½	**tsp ground cardamon**
½	**tsp ground coriander**
½	**tsp ground cumin**
	Grated rind and juice of 1 lemon

Add these five ingredients, stirring to blend well. Replace chicken, covering it with bulgur mixture.

At this point you may stop and continue later.

Cooking ...

3 **cups chicken broth, boiling**

Over contents of casserole, pour broth. Bake, covered, at 350° for 1 hour, or until chicken is tender.

Serve with ... Mixed Green Salad (p. 129)

Chicken with Cabbage

French

Here is a substantial and appetizing country dish which the gardener's wife at "La Domerie" (see Chicken with Apples), made for us one fall evening to eat in front of the fireplace. You will not, however, need a fireplace to appreciate its goodness!

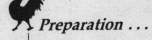

You will need ...	Preparation ...
	Assemble and prepare all ingredients.
2 Tbs butter 2 Tbs oil Serving-pieces of chicken for 6 persons Salt Pepper	In casserole, heat butter and oil and brown chicken; season. Remove.
3 medium potatoes, quartered	To remaining fat, add potatoes, turning to coat well; glaze slightly. Remove.
3 onions, chopped 3 Tbs parsley, chopped	In fat, cook onion until translucent. A little butter may be added if necessary. Add parsley. Replace chicken.
3 carrots, grated 1 small cabbage, shredded (about 4 cups) 1 tsp salt ¼ tsp pepper	To contents of casserole, add in layers carrot and cabbage; sprinkle with salt and pepper. At this point you may stop and continue later.

Cooking ...

1 cup white wine	Over contents of casserole, pour wine. Over cabbage, arrange reserved potatoes. Bake, covered, at 350° for 1 hour, or until chicken and potatoes are tender.

Serve with ... Green Salad with White Grapes (p. 128)

Chicken with Carrots

French

The sour cream-white wine sauce is delicate, flavored by the sweetness of the carrots. If desired, twelve peeled silver onions may be added.

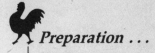

You will need ...	Preparation ...
	Assemble and prepare all ingredients.
¼ lb. salt pork, diced	In casserole, render salt pork until crisp; remove to absorbent paper. Reserve.
Serving-pieces of chicken for 6 persons Salt Pepper	In remaining fat, brown chicken; season. Remove. Discard excess fat.
½ cup white wine 2 bay leaves 1 clove garlic, minced	Add wine and deglaze casserole. Add bay leaves and garlic. Replace chicken.
1 cup white wine 1 cup sour cream ½ cup chicken broth	Combine these three ingredients, stirring to blend well; pour over chicken.
6 large carrots, scraped and thinly sliced 12 silver onions, peeled (optional)	Over contents of casserole, arrange in layers carrots, onions, and reserved pork bits.
	At this point you may stop and continue later.

Cooking ...

Bake, covered, at 350° for 1 hour, or until chicken and carrots are tender.

Serve with ... New Potatoes (p. 117) *or*
Noodles (p. 116)
Mixed Green Salad (p. 129)

Chicken with Chick-Peas—I

Indian

Curry is the distinctive flavor in this one-dish meal.

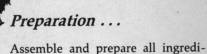

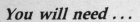

You will need . . .

Preparation . . .

Assemble and prepare all ingredients.

2 Tbs butter
2 Tbs oil
   Serving-pieces of chicken
      for 6 persons

In casserole, heat butter and oil and brown chicken. Remove.

2 onions, chopped

In remaining fat, cook onion until translucent.

3 Tbs flour
2 Tbs curry powder (or more,
      to taste)
1 tsp ground ginger
2 tsp salt

Combine flour with dry seasonings and add to onion, stirring to blend well.

6 Tbs honey
4 Tbs soy sauce
3 cups chicken broth

Combine liquids and add to contents of casserole. Cook over high heat, stirring, until sauce thickens.

At this point you may stop and continue later.

2 20-oz. cans chick-peas,
      drained

Add chick-peas to sauce. Replace chicken.

Cooking . . .

Bake, covered, at 350° for 1 hour, or until chicken is tender.

Serve with . . . Green Salad with White Grapes (p. 128)

Chicken with Chick-Peas—II

Indian

Coriander and cumin are the distinctive flavors in this recipe, which I often double and occasionally triple for buffet suppers.

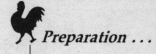

You will need ...   Preparation ...

Assemble and prepare all ingredients.

2 **Tbs butter** 2 **Tbs oil** **Serving-pieces of chicken for 6 persons** **Salt** **Pepper**	In casserole, heat butter and oil and brown chicken; season lightly. Remove.
3 **onions, chopped**	Cook onion until translucent.
1 **20-oz. can chick-peas, drained** 1 **tsp salt** ½ **tsp pepper** ¾ **tsp ginger** 1 **tsp (generous) ground cumin** 1 **Tbs ground coriander** 2 **Tbs chopped ginger root (optional)**	Add chick-peas and seasonings; cook, covered, over low heat for 10 minutes. Stir to blend mixture. Replace chicken, covering with chick-pea mixture. At this point you may stop and continue later.

Cooking ...

1½ **cups chicken broth, boiling**

Over contents of casserole, pour broth; bake, covered, at 350° for 1 hour, or until chicken is tender. Remove, cover and allow sauce to cook down (about 15 minutes more).

Serve with ... Mixed Green Salad (p. 129)

Chicken with Chick-Peas—III

Middle Eastern

Although the original recipe is complicated, this simplified version loses none of the flavor of the exotic Syrian soup-stew.

You will need . . .

Preparation . . .

Assemble and prepare all ingredients.

2	**Tbs butter**
2	**Tbs oil**
	Serving-pieces of chicken for 6 persons

In casserole, heat butter and oil and brown chicken. Remove.

1	**onion, chopped**

Discard all but 2 Tbs fat; in it, cook onion until translucent.

¾	**tsp chili powder**
½	**tsp ginger**
2	**tsp paprika**
½	**tsp turmeric**
1½	**tsp salt**
½	**tsp pepper**
1	**tsp sugar**
2	**Tbs minced parsley**
	Grated rind and juice of 1 lemon

To onion, add these ten ingredients, stirring to blend well.

3	**cups chicken broth**
2	**Tbs cornstarch**

Combine broth and cornstarch, stirring until smooth. Add to contents of casserole and cook over high heat until mixture thickens.

At this point you may stop and continue later.

1	**1-lb. can Italian tomatoes**
1	**20-oz. can chick-peas, with liquid**

To contents of casserole, add tomatoes and chick-peas, stirring. Replace chicken.

Cooking . . .

Bake, covered, at 350° for 1 hour, or until chicken is tender. Serve in soup bowls.

Serve with . . . Cucumber Salad (p. 127)

Chicken with Chili—I

Ethiopian

Like many dishes requiring several strong spices, this one is of elusive flavor.

You will need ...

Preparation ...

Assemble and prepare all ingredients.

2	**Tbs butter**
2	**Tbs oil**
	Serving-pieces of chicken for 6 persons

In casserole, heat butter and oil and brown chicken. Remove.

6	**onions, chopped**
1	**3" piece stick cinnamon**

In remaining fat, cook onions until translucent. Add cinnamon stick.

	Grated rind and juice of 1 lemon
4	**Tbs tomato paste**
2	**Tbs chili powder**
1	**tsp ginger**
1	**tsp salt**
½	**tsp pepper**
½	**cup red wine**
1½	**cups chicken broth**
2	**Tbs cornstarch**

Combine and blend well these ten ingredients.

2	**Tbs chopped fresh ginger root (optional)**

To onions, add liquid mixture and cook over high heat, stirring, until sauce thickens. (Sauce will not be heavy; for thicker sauce, use an additional Tbs cornstarch.) Add ginger root. Replace chicken.

At this point you may stop and continue later.

Cooking ...

Bake, covered, at 350° for 1 hour, or until chicken is tender.

Serve with ... Bulgur (p. 115)
Mixed Green Salad (p. 129)

Chicken with Chili—II

Jamaican

Though I prefer the Ethiopian chicken with chili, this Jamaican variation can be made easily from ingredients you probably have handy.

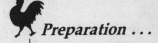

You will need ...	Preparation ...
	Assemble and prepare all ingredients.
Seasoned flour **Serving-pieces of chicken** **for 6 persons** 2 **Tbs butter** 2 **Tbs oil**	In seasoned flour, dredge chicken pieces. In casserole, heat butter and oil and brown chicken.
2 **onions, chopped** 2 **cloves garlic, chopped** 1½ **tsp poultry seasoning** 4 **Tbs soy sauce** 6 **Tbs tomato puree** 2 **Tbs chili powder** 1 **cup medium-dry sherry**	Combine these seven ingredients, stirring to blend mixture well. At this point you may stop and continue later.
	## Cooking ...
	Over contents of casserole, pour liquid mixture; bake, covered, at 350° for 1 hour, or until chicken is tender.

Serve with ... Rice (p. 115)
             or
             Corn Muffins (p. 122)
             Green Salad with White Grapes (p. 128)

Chicken with Chocolate Sauce

Mexican

Chicken *mole,* chicken with chocolate sauce, is a classic Mexican dish. The almonds may be omitted in favor of crushed peanuts; if desired, both may be used. Similarly nuts and/or raisins may be omitted entirely.

You will need . . .   *Preparation . . .*

	Assemble and prepare all ingredients.
4 Tbs olive oil 2 cloves garlic, minced Serving-pieces of chicken for 6 persons	In casserole, heat oil and cook garlic for a few minutes to flavor oil; add chicken and brown. Remove.
1 onion, chopped 1 green pepper, chopped 3 slices canned pimento, chopped 2 large tomatoes, peeled, seeded, and chopped	In remaining fat, cook onion, pepper, pimento, and tomato over gentle heat for 10 minutes.
2 Tbs chili powder 2½ cups chicken broth ¼ cup slivered almonds ¼ cup seedless raisins ½ tsp cumin seed ¼ tsp nutmeg ¼ tsp ground clove ¼ tsp cinnamon ½ tsp salt ¼ tsp pepper 1 tsp sugar Grated rind of 1 orange	To onion mixture, add chili powder, stirring to blend well. Add broth, almonds, raisins, seasonings, and rind, simmer, covered, for 30 minutes.
2 squares bitter chocolate, coarsely chopped	Add chocolate, stirring until melted. Replace chicken, spooning sauce over. At this point you may stop and continue later.

continued . . .

Cooking ...

¼ cup light rum

Bake, covered, at 350° for 1 hour, or until chicken is tender. Warm rum, ignite it, and pour over contents of casserole; allow to stand for a few minutes.

Serve with ... Brown Rice (p. 115)
Beans in Garlic Oil (p. 127) *or*
Spinach Salad with watercress (p. 131)

Chicken with Coriander—I

Indian

Here is a particularly tasty curry sauce which you make up from your own spice shelf, without relying on commercial curry powder. Despite the number of strong flavors at work, the dish is mild and subtle.

You will need ... 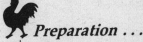 *Preparation ...*

Assemble and prepare all ingredients.

2 Tbs butter
2 Tbs oil
   Serving-pieces of chicken for 6 persons
   Salt
   Pepper

In casserole, heat butter and oil and brown chicken; season. Remove.

3 onions, chopped
1 clove garlic, chopped
3 Tbs ground coriander
1 tsp ginger
¼ tsp red pepper flakes
1 tsp sugar
½ tsp turmeric
1 cup chicken broth
1 cup yogurt

In remaining fat, cook onion and garlic until translucent. Add seasonings and stir to blend mixture. Add chicken broth and yogurt, stirring, and simmer for 5 minutes. Replace chicken.

At this point you may stop and continue later.

Cooking ...

Bake, covered, at 350° for 1 hour, or until chicken is tender.

Serve with ... Rice (p. 115)
Spinach Salad with mushrooms (p. 131)

Chicken with Coriander—II

Indian

Because of the difference in preparation and flavorings, this recipe is quite removed from the preceding one.

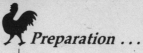

You will need ...

Preparation ...

Assemble and prepare all ingredients.

3 cups yogurt
Juice of 2 lemons
2 tsp salt
¾ tsp red pepper flakes
2 Tbs ground coriander
1 tsp ground cumin
1 tsp dried mint, finely crumbled

In blender, combine these seven ingredients and blend at low speed for 15 seconds.

Serving-pieces of chicken for 6 persons

In yogurt mixture, marinate chicken for 24 to 48 hours; place in refrigerator after first 4 hours. (The longer the marination, the tastier the dish.)

2 Tbs butter
2 Tbs oil

In casserole, heat butter and oil and brown chicken. (Scrape excess marinade from chicken and dry on absorbent paper; marinade burns easily.) Pour remaining marinade over browned chicken.

At this point you may stop and continue later.

Cooking ...

Bake, covered, at 350° for 1 hour, or until chicken is tender.

Serve with ... Rice (p. 115)
Spinach Salad with watercress and mushrooms (p. 131)

Chicken with Cream—I

American

Very easy, *very* good, and VERY rich! The source of this recipe is my great-great grandmother, who lived on a farm where she raised a large family and where, in an era of readily available domestic help, she had several servants. Dinner, always a noon meal, was cleared away by the family as well as by the maids, and, when all was tidied, Great-great Grandmother and the three maid-servants retired to their respective rooms, changed into tea frocks, and met again in the dining room. Here, over tea and polite conversation, Great-great Grandmother taught girls how to sew. She took a motherly interest in them and in their "domestic education," and in later years spoke of the "very suitable marriages my girls have made."

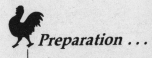

You will need ...

Seasoned flour
1 tsp celery salt
1 tsp paprika
   Serving-pieces of chicken
      for 6 persons
2 Tbs butter
2 Tbs oil

½ lb. mushrooms, quartered
      and sautéed in butter
      for 5 minutes (op-
      tional)
2 cups medium cream

Preparation ...

Assemble and prepare all ingredients.

To seasoned flour, add celery salt and paprika. In flour mixture, dredge chicken. In casserole, heat butter and oil and brown chicken.

At this point you may stop and continue later.

To contents of casserole, add mushrooms (if desired) and cream.

Cooking ...

Bake, covered, at 350° for 1 hour, or until chicken is tender.

Serve with ... Barley (p. 115)
                 Artichokes (p. 127)

Chicken with Cream—II

American

Similar in preparation to Chicken with Fresh Tarragon, this dish is especially appropriate for supper parties.

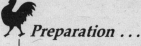

You will need ...

Seasoned flour
Serving-pieces of chicken
    for 6 persons
2 Tbs butter
2 Tbs oil

½ cup cognac

1 8-oz. package cream
    cheese, coarsely
    chopped
1 cup milk, scalded
½ cup white wine
3 onions, chopped

½ cup grated or finely
    chopped Muenster
    cheese

Preparation ...

Assemble and prepare all ingredients.

In seasoned flour, dredge chicken. In casserole, heat butter and oil and brown chicken. Discard any remaining seasoned flour.

Warm cognac, ignite, and pour over chicken.

At this point you may stop and continue later.

In blender, combine these four ingredients and blend on low speed for 15 seconds, or until smooth. Pour sauce over chicken.

Cooking ...

Bake, covered, at 350° for 1 hour, or until chicken is tender. Sprinkle over cheese and place under broiler until cheese browns slightly.

Variations: In place of onion, 8 scallions, diagonally sliced, may be used (do not put in blender). If desired, ½ lb. mushrooms, sliced and sautéed, may be added to chicken before sauce is poured over.

Serve with ... Bulgur (p. 115) *or* Cream biscuits (p. 123)
Watercress Salad with parsley and red onion (p. 132)

Chicken with Currants

American

Pineapple, cinnamon, clove, and orange are the flavoring agents of this fresh-tasting dish.

You will need ...

	Seasoned flour
	Serving-pieces of chicken for 6 persons
2	**Tbs butter**
2	**Tbs oil**
½	**cup slivered almonds, toasted**
½	**cup currants (or seedless raisins)**
1	**cup crushed pineapple, with juice**
½	**tsp cinnamon**
¼	**tsp clove**
	Grated rind of 1 orange
1	**clove garlic**
2½	**cups orange juice**

Preparation ...

Assemble and prepare all ingredients.

In seasoned flour, dredge chicken. In casserole, heat butter and oil and brown chicken.

To contents of casserole, add these six ingredients.

Put garlic through press into orange juice; stir to blend well.

At this point you may stop and continue later.

Cooking ...

Over contents of casserole, pour orange juice. Bake, covered, at 350° for 1 hour, or until chicken is tender.

Serve with ... Rice (p. 115)
Spinach Salad (p. 131)

Chicken with Curry
Indian

Indian curries are hot and their sauces are frequently unthickened. In America, a less aromatic curry dish is usually preferred, with a thickened sauce. The amount of curry powder suggested here is for the fairly brave; use more or less, as your taste dictates. The sauce, while thickened, is not heavy; it can be made thicker or thinner by use of more or less flour.

You will need ... | Preparation ...

	Assemble and prepare all ingredients.
2 Tbs butter 2 Tbs oil Serving-pieces of chicken for 6 persons Salt Pepper	In casserole, heat butter and oil and brown chicken; season. Remove.
8 to 12 scallions, sliced diagonally (with as much green as possible) ½ cup chopped fresh parsley	In remaining fat, sauté scallions and parsley for 5 minutes.
1½ Tbs curry powder 1 tsp paprika ½ tsp powdered basil *or* thyme ¾ tsp salt ¼ cup flour	Add seasonings, stirring to blend well. Then add flour, stirring.
1 cup hot milk 1 cup chicken broth 1 1-lb. can Italian tomatoes	Add in succession, milk, chicken broth, and tomatoes, stirring constantly until sauce thickens.
⅓ cup currants ½ cup seedless raisins ½ cup chopped almonds 1 4-oz. jar pimento, chopped	Add these four ingredients, stirring to blend well.
	At this point you may stop and continue later.

continued . . .

Cooking ...

Replace chicken. Bake, covered, at 350° for 1 hour, or until chicken is tender.

Serve with ...Rice (p. 115) and condiments for curry (p. 5)
Green Salad with White Grapes (p. 128)

Chicken with Dates

Middle Eastern

This Syrian dish may be garnished with oranges, sliced paper-thin and seeded.

You will need ...

Preparation ...

Assemble and prepare all ingredients.

2 Tbs butter	In casserole, heat butter and oil and brown chicken; season. Remove. Discard excess fat.
2 Tbs oil	
Serving-pieces of chicken for 6 persons	
Salt	
Pepper	

Combine these eight ingredients, mix well, and, in casserole over high heat, cook, stirring, until sauce thickens. Replace chicken.

1 cup orange juice
2 cups chicken broth
3 Tbs cornstarch
1 tsp salt
½ tsp pepper
1 tsp curry powder
1 onion, chopped
Juice of 1 lemon

At this point you may stop and continue later.

Cooking ...

Bake, covered, at 350° for 45 minutes.

12 to 18 dates, pitted and cut in halves lengthwise
1 green pepper, chopped

On top of chicken, arrange dates. Sprinkle with green pepper (garnish with orange slices, if desired), and continue to bake, covered, for 15 minutes, or until chicken is tender.

Serve with ... Rice (p. 115) *or*
French Bread (p. 120)
Lentils with Oil and Lemon (p. 129)

Chicken with Dumplings

American

Sometimes this dish is called "chicken fricasee" and sometimes "smothered chicken." For another chicken-with-dumplings recipe, see Chicken with Milk. This recipe comes from Grandmother Boucher, a Missouri farm woman of diminutive height but impressive weight. When she was young, farmsteads in Missouri were far from stores and supplies. Folks feeling lonely went calling, frequently journeying many miles. For this reason, the visited would have to provide at least one big meal. Therefore, Grandmother Boucher kept a well-stocked larder from which she could make any number of good dishes. She cooked for a family of men and boys; no girls had been born for several generations. Her husband and sons consumed with relish, at one meal, as much as Grandmother Boucher, despite her rotundity, required in a week.

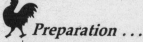

You will need ...   Preparation ...

Assemble and prepare all ingredients.

6	Tbs butter
6	Tbs flour
4	cups chicken broth, boiling

In casserole, melt butter and add flour. Cook gently for 5 minutes, stirring. Increase heat and, when mixture foams, add broth, stirring constantly until sauce is smooth and thick.

	Serving-pieces of chicken for 6 persons
2	onions, chopped
2	stalks celery, chopped
1	tsp sugar
2	tsp salt
8	peppercorns
1	tsp basil *or* sage *or* thyme
2	bay leaves
6	whole cloves
1	clove garlic, minced
½	cup parsley, chopped *or* 1 Tbs chives, chopped

To sauce, add chicken, onion, celery, and seasonings.

At this point you may stop and continue later.

Cooking ...

Bake, covered, at 350° for 40 minutes.

1	10-oz. package frozen peas and carrots (optional)

If desired, add vegetables, stirring them into sauce. Cover and continue cooking for 5 minutes.

continued ...

Add dumpling dough of your choice (see Dumplings, p. 152) and cook, covered, for 20 minutes; do NOT remove cover for these 20 minutes. Dumplings do NOT freeze.

Serve with ... Mixed Green Salad (p. 129)

Chicken with Eggplant—I

Italian

Despite its ease of preparation, this dish is redolent of Italy and the friendly small restaurants of Rome.

You will need ...   **Preparation ...**

Assemble and prepare all ingredients.

4 Tbs olive oil Serving-pieces of chicken for 6 persons Salt Pepper	In casserole, heat oil and brown chicken; season. Remove.
1 large eggplant, peeled and cubed 2 onions, chopped 1 clove garlic, minced	Into remaining fat, stir eggplant, onion, and garlic; cook, covered, for 10 minutes, stirring frequently. If necessary, add more oil.
3 Tbs flour 1½ cups chicken broth ½ cup red wine	Stir in flour; add broth and wine and cook, stirring, until mixture thickens. Replace chicken.
	At this point you may stop and continue later.

Cooking ...

Pimento, chopped, as garnish (optional)   Bake, covered, at 350° for 1 hour, or until chicken is tender. (Pimento may be added for final 5 minutes of cooking.)

Serve with ... Noodles (p. 116)
Mixed Green Salad (p. 129)

Chicken with Eggplant—II

Italian

This second Italian recipe for chicken with eggplant is not a variation of the first; it is a lighter dish, more delicately flavored.

You will need . . .	*Preparation . . .*
	Assemble and prepare all ingredients.
2 Tbs butter	In casserole, heat butter and oil and brown chicken; season.
2 Tbs oil	
Serving-pieces of chicken for 6 persons	
Salt	
Pepper	
¼ lb. mushrooms, sliced	To contents of casserole, add in layers these five ingredients.
1 medium eggplant, peeled and cut into strips	
2 tomatoes, peeled, seeded, and chopped	
½ green pepper, chopped	
12 white onions, peeled	
¼ tsp basil	Combine seasonings and sprinkle over vegetables.
¼ tsp thyme	
½ tsp salt	At this point you may stop and continue later.
1 tsp sugar	
	Cooking . . .
1½ cups dry white wine	Pour wine over contents of casserole; bake, covered, at 350° for 1 hour, or until chicken is tender.

Serve with . . . Lentils with Oil and Lemon (p. 129)

Chicken with Eggplant—III

Middle Eastern (Lebanese)

The wine is my addition; if desired, you may substitute chicken broth. (Like many dishes from the Levant which can be made with different meats, this one is good prepared with beef or lean lamb: allow about ½ lb. of cubed meat per person, use red wine rather than white, and increase the cooking time to approximately 2½ hours.)

You will need ... 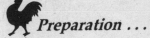	*Preparation ...*
	Assemble and prepare all ingredients.
2 **Tbs butter** 2 **Tbs oil** **Serving-pieces of chicken for 6 persons** **Salt** **Pepper**	In casserole, heat butter and oil and brown chicken; season. Remove.
3 **onions, chopped** 1 **green pepper, chopped (optional)** ¼ **lb. mushrooms, sliced (optional)** 1 **large eggplant, cubed**	In remaining fat, cook onion and pepper until translucent. Stir in mushrooms and cook 5 minutes. Stir in eggplant and cook 5 minutes.
1 **tsp paprika** 1 **tsp ground allspice** ½ **tsp cumin seed (optional)** 1 **tsp salt** ½ **tsp pepper** 1 **tsp sugar**	Add seasonings and stir to blend mixture. Replace chicken, covering with eggplant mixture. At this point you may stop and continue later.
	### *Cooking ...*
1 **1-lb. can Italian tomatoes (with liquid)** 1 **cup dry white wine**	Over contents of casserole, pour tomatoes and wine. Bake, covered, at 350° for 1 hour, or until chicken is tender. (The dish should be moist but not liquid.)

Serve with ... Corn Muffins (p. 122)
Spinach Salad with water chestnuts (p. 131)

Chicken with Garlic Sauce

French

The sauce is *not* overpowering. To the contrary, it is delicate—and *very* good!

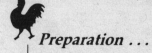

You will need ...	**Preparation ...**
	Assemble and prepare all ingredients.
Seasoned flour Serving-pieces of chicken for 6 persons 2 Tbs butter 2 Tbs oil	In seasoned flour, dredge chicken. In casserole, heat butter and oil and brown chicken. Remove.
1½ cups dry white wine 1½ cups chicken broth	To casserole, add any remaining flour, stirring to blend well. Add wine and deglaze casserole. Add broth and cook, stirring, until sauce thickens.
15 to 20 garlic cloves, peeled and cut in lengthwise halves ½ cup parsley, chopped 1 tsp dried tarragon	Stir in these three ingredients. Replace chicken. At this point you may stop and continue later. ## Cooking ... Bake, covered, at 350° for 1 hour, or until chicken is tender.

Serve with ... Barley (p. 115)
Mushrooms with herbs (p. 130)
or
Green Salad with White Grapes (p. 128)

Chicken with Garum Sauce

Italian (Roman)

Garum, a seasoning agent used in ancient Roman cookery, was the pickling brine derived from salting seawater fish and squeezing them to extract the liquid. It was sometimes put in little pots, as mustard is today; this *garum nigrum* could then be seasoned according to individual taste with vinegar, oil, or pepper. The present recipe approximates *garum* sauce with present-day ingredients.

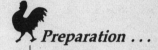

You will need ... Preparation ...

Assemble and prepare all ingredients.

2 **Tbs butter**	In casserole, heat butter and oil and brown chicken, dredged in flour. Discard excess fat.
2 **Tbs oil**	
Serving-pieces of chicken for 6 persons	
Flour	

1 **10½-oz. can chicken broth**	In blender, combine these 6 ingredients; blend on low speed for 15 seconds.
3 **Tbs Madeira wine**	
½ **cup evaporated milk**	
1 **tsp (generous) anchovy paste**	At this point you may stop and continue later.
¼ **tsp pepper**	
1 **tsp ground cumin**	

Cooking ...

Over contents of casserole, pour blended sauce; bake, covered, at 350° for 1 hour, or until chicken is tender.

Serve with ...
Rice (p. 115)
or
Spaghetti (p. 116)
Mixed Green Salad (p. 129)

Chicken with Ginger—I

Hawaiian

I first enjoyed this recipe at the home of Joji Wago, a designer in Honolulu who created the stage settings for the Honolulu Opera Festival while I was engaged as the stage director. It is hard to say which is more tasteful, Mr. Wago's theatrical design or his cooking.

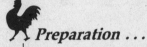

You will need ...	*Preparation* ...
	Assemble and prepare all ingredients.
2 **Tbs butter**	In casserole, heat butter and oil and brown chicken; season. Remove. Discard excess fat.
2 **Tbs oil**	
Serving-pieces of chicken for 6 persons	
Salt	
Pepper	
1½ **cups chicken broth**	Combine broth, juice, jam, and soy sauce; stir to dissolve jam. If necessary, add water to equal 3 cups. Stir in cornstarch. Add to casserole and cook, stirring constantly, until sauce thickens.
Pineapple juice reserved from 1 20-oz. can pineapple chunks	
4 **Tbs plum jam or jelly**	
4 **Tbs soy sauce**	
Water	
3 **Tbs cornstarch**	
Reserved pineapple chunks	Stir these three ingredients into sauce. Replace chicken.
¼ **cup fresh ginger root, diced**	At this point you may stop and continue later.
¾ **cup blanched slivered almonds**	

Cooking ...

Bake, covered, at 350° for 1 hour, or until chicken is tender.

Serve with ... Rice (p. 115)
Salad of your choice

Chicken with Ginger—II
Malayan

This recipe is less gingery than the previous one, and because of the various seasonings, it may perhaps be subtler.

You will need ...	*Preparation ...*
	Assemble and prepare all ingredients.
4 onions, coarsely chopped 2 cloves garlic 1 Tbs salt 2 tsp sugar ½ tsp powdered clove 1 tsp ground coriander 1 Tbs powdered ginger ½ tsp red pepper flakes	In blender, combine these eight ingredients and reduce to a liquid paste.
Serving-pieces of chicken for 6 persons	In onion-spice mixture, marinate chicken for 4 hours.
	Remove chicken from marinade and wipe clean; reserve marinade.
2 Tbs butter 2 Tbs oil	In casserole, heat butter and oil and brown chicken.
Juice and grated rind of 1 lemon 3 Tbs plum jam or jelly 1 cup boiling water	Combine reserved marinade with these four ingredients. Pour over chicken.
	At this point you may stop and continue later.
	Cooking ...
	Bake, covered, at 350° for 1 hour, or until chicken is tender.

Serve with ... Rice *or* Bulgur (p. 115)
Oriental Salad (p. 130)

Chicken with Grapes

French

An unusually delicate dish, particularly welcome for light dining.

You will need ...

Preparation ...

Assemble and prepare all ingredients.

	Seasoned flour
	Serving-pieces of chicken for 6 persons
2	Tbs butter
2	Tbs oil

In seasoned flour, dredge chicken. In casserole, heat butter and oil and brown chicken. Remove.

1½	cups white wine
1	cup chicken broth

To casserole, add 1 Tbs remaining seasoned flour, stirring. Add wine, stirring and scraping to deglaze casserole. Add broth and, over high heat, cook, stirring, until sauce thickens. Replace chicken.

At this point you may stop and continue later.

Cooking ...

Bake, covered, at 350° for 45 minutes.

½	cup toasted slivered almonds
½	lb. (or more, to taste) seedless white grapes, washed and well drained

Add almonds and then grapes. Cook, covered, 15 minutes longer, or until chicken is tender.

Serve with ... Rice (p. 115)
Mixed Green Salad (p. 129)

Chicken with Green Peas

Portuguese

Cool to look at and delicate to taste, this recipe is ideal for spring and summer menus. Fresh peas may be substituted for the frozen; the lettuce turns into a puree.

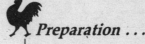

You will need ... Preparation ...

Assemble and prepare all ingredients.

Seasoned flour Serving-pieces of chicken for 6 persons 2 Tbs butter 2 Tbs oil	In seasoned flour, dredge chicken. In casserole, heat butter and oil and brown chicken (add more butter and oil, if necessary). Remove.
3 onions, chopped 1 carrot, thinly sliced 1 bay leaf, broken ¼ tsp powdered clove ¼ tsp marjoram ¼ tsp thyme Dash cayenne 2 Tbs of remaining seasoned flour	In remaining fat, cook onion and carrot for a few minutes, stirring to coat well. Add seasonings. Stir in flour.
1 large head tender lettuce, washed, dried, and shredded	Over contents of casserole, arrange lettuce in a layer. Replace chicken. At this point you may stop and continue later.

Cooking ...

2 10-oz. packages frozen peas	Bake, covered, at 350° for 45 minutes. Add peas and continue to bake, covered, for 15 minutes, or until chicken and peas are tender. If desired, the completed dish may be garnished with chopped fresh dill, mint, or tarragon.

Serve with ... New Potatoes (p. 117)
Mushrooms with Herbs (p. 130)

Chicken with Green Peppers

Italian

A delicate, fresh-tasting dish, especially suited to light meals.

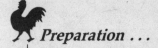

You will need ...	**Preparation ...**
	Assemble and prepare all ingredients.
4 **Tbs olive oil** **Serving-pieces of chicken** **for 6 persons** **Salt** **Pepper**	In casserole, heat oil and brown chicken; season. Remove.
4 **green peppers, seeded and** **sliced**	In fat, sauté pepper until limp. Remove.
1 **onion, chopped** 1 **clove garlic, chopped**	In remaining fat, cook onion and garlic until translucent.
1 **cup dry white wine**	Add wine and cook until liquid is reduced by half.
3 **large ripe tomatoes,** **peeled, seeded, and** **chopped**	Add tomatoes, stirring to blend mixture. Replace chicken, spooning sauce over. Top with peppers.
	At this point you may stop and continue later.

Cooking ...

Bake, covered, at 350° for 1 hour, or until chicken is tender.

Serve with ... Rice (p. 115)
Mixed Green Salad with mushrooms (p. 129)

Chicken with Herbs

French

It is important that the herbs be garden-fresh. If the reader is as en-
thusiastic about the recipe as I am, he may well be led to start a few
pots of herbs on a window sill. Basil, chive, dill, marjoram, parsley, and
tarragon are very useful, easily grown herbs. Known in France as *poulet
au vert* (literally, chicken in the green), this dish is remarkably fresh.

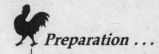

You will need ...

Preparation ...

Assemble and prepare all ingredients.

2	Tbs butter
2	Tbs oil
	Serving-pieces of chicken for 6 persons
	Salt
	Pepper

In casserole, heat butter and oil and
brown chicken; season. Remove.

4   Tbs flour

To remaining fat, add flour, stirring,
and cook gently 5 minutes.

1½ cups milk
1½ cups chicken broth

Combine liquids and heat, bringing
nearly to the boil; add to flour mixture and, over high heat, cook, stirring, until sauce thickens.

1   generous Tbs each:
     basil, celery leaves, cher-
       vil, chive, dill,
       marjoram, parsley,
       tarragon *or* sage
½ tsp dried thyme

Chop fresh herbs and stir into sauce;
add thyme.

At this point you may stop and continue later.

Cooking ...

Replace chicken. Bake, covered, at
350° for 1 hour, or until chicken is
tender.

Serve with ... French Bread (p. 120)
                    Spinach Salad with mushrooms (p. 131)

Chicken with Honey

Moroccan

While I find this dish delicious, it *is* sweeter than most Occidental meat recipes. Try it privately or serve it to adventurous friends.

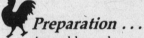

You will need . . .	Preparation . . .
	Assemble and prepare all ingredients.
2 **Tbs butter** 2 **Tbs oil** **Serving-pieces of chicken for 6 persons** **Salt** **Pepper**	In casserole, heat butter and oil and brown chicken; season. Remove.
2 **onions, chopped** 1 **clove garlic, chopped**	In remaining fat, cook onion and garlic until translucent.
1 **cup ground almonds** 1 **Tbs sweet basil, dried** ½ **tsp pepper** ½ **cup honey**	Add these four ingredients and, over gentle heat, cook, stirring, until mixture is well blended.
1½ **cups chicken broth** 2 **Tbs cornstarch** **Juice of 1 lemon**	Combine broth and cornstarch and add to contents of casserole; over high heat, cook, stirring, until sauce thickens. Remove from heat, stir in lemon juice, and replace chicken, spooning sauce over.
	At this point you may stop and continue later.

Cooking . . .

Bake, covered, at 350° for 1 hour, or until chicken is tender.

Serve with . . . Bulgur (p. 115)
Watercress Salad with parsley and red onion (p. 132)

Chicken with Horseradish

Flemish

This dish is frequently found in Europe; I have never seen it in America, however. I found the recipe at a restaurant in Bruges, Belgium. Bruges, during the thirteenth and fourteenth centuries one of Europe's most important commercial cities, remains unspoiled today. A city of only 52,000 people, built on canals where swans glide gracefully, it boasts some of the most interesting architecture I know. At one time capital of the court of Burgundy and birthplace of the Flemish painters Memling and Van Eyck, Bruges is still graced by the guildhouses and consulates of early Renaissance foreign merchants. On a recent trip there, I stayed at the Hotel Duc de Bourgogne, where my room overlooked a canal, the swans, and a picturesque corner of the town. The restaurant of the hotel, commanding the same vista, served excellent food.

You will need ... 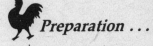 *Preparation ...*

		Assemble and prepare all ingredients.
2	Tbs butter	In casserole, heat butter and oil and brown chicken; season. Remove.
2	Tbs oil	
	Serving-pieces of chicken for 6 persons	
	Salt	
	Pepper	
4	Tbs flour	To remaining fat, add flour and cook gently for 5 minutes, stirring.
1½	cups milk	Combine liquids and heat, bringing nearly to the boil. Add to flour mixture and, over high heat, cook, stirring until sauce is thickened.
1½	cups chicken broth	
⅓	cup raisins *or* currants	Stir in raisins and seasonings.
1	Tbs lemon juice	At this point you may stop and continue later.
1	tsp sugar	
5	Tbs prepared horseradish	

Cooking ...

Replace chicken. Bake, covered, at 350° for 1 hour, or until chicken is tender.

Serve with ... New Potatoes (p. 117) *or*
                Potato Pancakes (p. 117)
                Green Bean Salad with red onion (p. 128)

Chicken with Lemon

American

This dish is a cheat! So easy to make and so elegant to serve. Good party fare.

You will need ... **Preparation ...**

	Assemble and prepare all ingredients.
Seasoned flour Serving-pieces of chicken for 6 persons 2 Tbs butter 2 Tbs oil	In seasoned flour, dredge chicken. In casserole, heat butter and oil and brown chicken. Remove.
2 onions, chopped ½ lb. mushrooms, sliced	In remaining fat, cook onions and mushrooms until onions are translucent.
1 tsp dry mustard 1 tsp dried sweet basil	To contents of casserole, add 3 Tbs remaining seasoned flour and seasonings, stirring.
1 cup light cream, scalded 1½ cups chicken broth ½ cup fresh lemon juice Grated rind of 1½ lemons	Combine liquid ingredients and add to contents of casserole; over high heat, cook, stirring, until sauce thickens.
	At this point you may stop and continue later.

Cooking ...

Replace chicken. Bake, covered, at 350° for 1 hour, or until chicken is tender.

Serve with ... New Potatoes (p. 117) *or* Brown Rice (p. 115)
Mixed Green Salad (p. 129)

Chicken with Lime

American

This light dish has a fresh taste, ideal for summer meals. The suggested menu is for such a supper, eaten leisurely in the cool of the day.

You will need ...

Juice of 3 limes
Juice of 1 lemon
½ cup dry white wine
1 tsp sugar
1 tsp salt
¼ tsp pepper
½ tsp dried tarragon, crumbled fine
1 clove garlic, pressed

Serving-pieces of chicken for 6 persons

2 Tbs butter
2 Tbs oil

Grated rind of 3 limes
1 Tbs cornstarch

Preparation ...

Assemble and prepare all ingredients.

Combine these eight ingredients to make marinade.

Marinate chicken, turning occasionally (4 hours at room temperature; up to 8 hours if refrigerated).

In casserole, heat butter and oil. Dry chicken on absorbent paper and brown lightly. Strain and reserve marinade.

At this point you may stop and continue later.

Cooking ...

To marinade, add grated rind and cornstarch, stirring until mixture is smooth. Pour over contents of casserole; bake, covered, at 350° for 1 hour, or until chicken is tender.

Serve with ...

Cream Biscuits (p. 123)
Green Bean Salad (p. 128)

Chicken with Liqueur

French

This dish, known in France as *poulet Rouennaise,* is good party fare; like Chicken with Lemon, it is elegant but easily made.

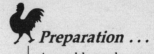

You will need ...

Preparation ...

Assemble and prepare all ingredients.

2 Tbs butter
2 Tbs oil
   Serving-pieces of chicken for 6 persons
   Salt
   Pepper

In casserole, heat butter and oil and brown chicken; season.

⅓ cup cognac *or* kirsch *or* orange-flavored liqueur

Warm liqueur, ignite, and pour over chicken. When flame dies, remove chicken.

½ lb. mushrooms, sliced (optional)

In casserole, cook mushrooms 5 minutes.

2 Tbs flour
2 cups light cream, scalded *or* 1 can evaporated milk and water to equal 2 cups
2 tsp tomato paste, for color (optional)

To contents of casserole, add flour, stirring to blend mixture. Add cream and tomato paste; over high heat, cook, stirring, until sauce thickens. Adjust seasoning.

At this point you may stop and continue later.

Cooking ...

Replace chicken. Bake, covered, at 350° for 1 hour, or until chicken is tender. If desired, garnish with sliced water chestnuts, pine nuts, or toasted slivered almonds.

***Serve with* ...** Noodles (p. 116)
Watercress Salad with parsley and red onion (p. 132)

Chicken with Milk

American

Slow, thorough browning of the chicken is all-important to the flavor of this mild dish, which is especially good with dumplings.

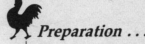

You will need ...

Preparation ...

Assemble and prepare all ingredients.

2	**Tbs butter**
2	**Tbs oil**
	Serving-pieces of chicken for 6 persons
	Salt
	Pepper

In casserole, heat butter and oil and brown chicken; season. Remove.

¼	**cup flour**
3½	**cups milk, scalded**

Discard all but 4 Tbs fat. To reserved fat, add flour and cook, stirring, over gentle heat for a few minutes. Add milk and, over high heat, cook, stirring, until sauce is thick and smooth.

At this point you may stop and continue later.

Cooking ...

¼ **cup chopped fresh parsley**

Replace chicken. Bake, covered, at 350° for 1 hour, or until chicken is tender. If desired, add dumpling dough (see p. 152) after first 40 minutes. Dish may be garnished with parsley.

Serve with ... Spinach Salad (p. 131)

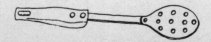

Chicken with Mincemeat

Indian

The native recipe calls for bits of meat—truly "minced meat"—in addition to fruit, but I have adapted it to ingredients readily available in our supermarkets. Perhaps this is the most popular of my chicken recipes: I am frequently, and flatteringly, asked to make it again by friends who have had it before.

You will need ...   *Preparation ...*

Assemble and prepare all ingredients.

2	Tbs butter
2	Tbs oil
1	clove garlic, minced
	Serving-pieces of chicken for 6 persons
	Salt
	Pepper

In casserole, heat butter and oil and cook garlic until golden. Add chicken and brown; season.

| 2 | 9-oz. packets concentrated (dehydrated) mincemeat |
| 2 | cups water |

Crumble mincemeat into saucepan. Add water and cook over high heat, stirring until lumps have disappeared. Boil for 1 minute.

3	onions, chopped
1	tsp curry powder
	Grated rind and juice of 1 lemon
2	tsp cider vinegar

To mincemeat, add these five ingredients, stirring to blend mixture.

At this point you may stop and continue later.

Cooking ...

Pour mincemeat mixture over chicken; bake, covered, at 350° for 1 hour, or until chicken is tender.

Serve with ... Rice (p. 115)
or
White Bread (p. 120)
Green Salad with White Grapes (p. 128)

Chicken
with Mint
Middle Eastern

This exotic dish requires *fresh* mint; dried mint will not substitute.

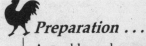

You will need ...	Preparation ...
	Assemble and prepare all ingredients.
Seasoned flour 1 tsp paprika Serving-pieces of chicken for 6 persons 2 Tbs butter 2 Tbs oil	To seasoned flour, add paprika; in flour mixture, dredge chicken. In casserole, heat butter and oil and brown chicken. Remove.
2 Tbs remaining seasoned flour 1 10½-oz. can chicken broth	In remaining fat, stir seasoned flour; add broth and cook, stirring, until sauce thickens.
Grated rind and juice of 1½ lemons 2 Tbs brown sugar 1 cup mint leaves, finely chopped ½ lemon, sliced paper thin, seeds removed.	Stir together lemon rind, juice, and sugar; add to sauce, together with mint, and stir to blend mixture. Replace chicken and spoon sauce over; top with layer of lemon slices. At this point, you may stop and continue later.

Cooking ...

Bake, covered, at 350° for 1 hour, or until chicken is tender.

Serve with ... Bulgur (p. 115)
Mixed Green Salad (p. 129)

Chicken with Mustard Sauce

French

Mlle. Masse, the source of this recipe, was a petite, prim maiden lady who lived in Tourcoing, France, near the Belgian border. Refusing to leave her family home during World Wars I and II, she protected her heirlooms, especially the silver pieces, by burying them. Later, in reduced circumstances, she rented two rooms of her house. Proud to the last, however, she required her boarders to wear "proper dress" for dinner. She always served dinner in the dining room, except in the winter of '55, when the temperature was often 20° below zero. During those grim days, she and her two boarders lived chiefly in the kitchen, the only room capable of being adequately heated and talked of food.

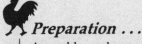

You will need . . .	*Preparation . . .*
	Assemble and prepare all ingredients.
2 **Tbs butter**	In casserole, heat butter and oil and
2 **Tbs oil**	brown chicken; season. Remove.
Serving-pieces of chicken for 6 persons	
Salt	
Pepper	
2 **onions, chopped**	In remaining fat, cook onion until translucent.
4 **Tbs flour**	To onion, add flour and turmeric
½ **tsp turmeric (optional)**	and cook gently, stirring, for 5 minutes.
1½ **cups milk**	Combine liquids and heat, bringing
1½ **cups chicken broth**	nearly to the boil. Add to onion mixture and cook, stirring, until sauce thickens.
	At this point you may stop and continue later.

Cooking . . .

Replace chicken. Bake, covered, at 350° for 1 hour, or until chicken is tender. Remove to warm serving plate.

3 **(generous) Tbs Dijon mustard**	To sauce, add mustard and parsley, stirring to blend mixture. Pour over
½ **cup chopped fresh parsley**	chicken and serve.

continued . . .

Variation: Chicken with Curry Sauce—omit mustard and turmeric; substitute 1 (generous) Tbs curry powder and 2 tsp sugar. It is unnecessary to remove chicken to warm plate. Parsley may be omitted, if desired. This variation is mine, not Mlle. Masse's; it goes well with rice, condiments for curries, and Oriental salad.

Serve with ... Noodles (p. 116)
Mixed Green Salad (p. 129)

Chicken with Onions—I

French

Called in France, *poulet à la lyonnaise,* this dish should be served with a bread to sop up the sauce.

You will need ...	*Preparation ...*
	Assemble and prepare all ingredients.
2 **Tbs butter** 2 **Tbs oil** **Serving-pieces of chicken for 6 persons** **Salt** **Pepper**	In casserole, heat butter and oil and brown chicken; season. Remove.
4 **large onions, sliced**	In remaining fat, cook onion until translucent.
2 **Tbs flour** 1 **10½-oz. can beef bouillon** ½ **cup dry red wine** **Water**	Add flour to casserole, stirring. Combine bouillon, wine, and water to equal two cups. Add to onion mixture and cook, stirring, until sauce thickens. Replace chicken.
	At this point you may stop and continue later.

Cooking ...

Bake, covered, at 350° for 1 hour, or until chicken is tender.

Serve with ... French Bread (p. 120)
Artichokes (p. 127)

Chicken with Onions—II

Greek

This *stifado*—stew made with onion—is flavorful but not too highly seasoned. The tomato paste and wine cook to a smooth sauce. In preparing the dish, occasionally spoon the sauce over the other ingredients to keep them moist.

You will need . . .

Preparation . . .

Assemble and prepare all ingredients.

2 **Tbs butter**	In casserole, heat butter and oil and
2 **Tbs oil**	brown chicken; season. Remove.
Serving-pieces of chicken	
for 6 persons	
Salt	
Pepper	

18 **small onions, peeled**   In remaining fat, glaze onions, stirring to coat well. Remove. Replace chicken.

1 **2" piece cinnamon stick**   Add cinnamon and cloves. Replace
8 **whole cloves**   onions. Sprinkle currants over all.
½ **cup currants** *or* **seedless raisins**

1 **cup red wine**   Combine these six ingredients,
2 **Tbs wine vinegar**   shaking or stirring to blend well.
1 **tsp ground cumin**   Pour sauce over contents of cas-
1 **tsp fenugreek (optional)**   serole.
1 **clove garlic, pressed**
1 **6-oz. can tomato paste**   At this point you may stop and continue later.

Cooking . . .

Bake, covered, at 350° for 1 hour, or until chicken is tender.

Serve with . . . Bulgur (p. 115)
Green Salad with White Grapes (p. 128)

Chicken with Oranges—I

American

There are several examples in this book of chicken combined with fruit, a custom which derives from Middle Eastern cooking. I feel it is one which should be more often emulated, and so have included the following recipe.

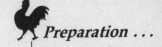

You will need ...

Seasoned flour
Serving-pieces of chicken
for 6 persons
2 Tbs butter
2 Tbs oil

1 onion, chopped
Celery seed

Grated rind of 1 orange
1½ cups orange juice
1 orange, unpeeled, sliced
paper thin, seeds
removed

Preparation ...

Assemble and prepare all ingredients.

In seasoned flour, dredge chicken. In casserole, heat butter and oil and brown chicken. Remove.

In remaining fat, cook onion until translucent. Replace chicken and sprinkle lightly with celery seed.

Over contents of casserole, sprinkle orange rind, pour orange juice, and arrange layer of orange slices.

At this point you may stop and continue later.

Cooking ...

Bake, covered, at 350° for 1 hour, or until chicken is tender.

Serve with ... Rice (p. 115)
or
Hominy (p. 118)
Watercress Salad (p. 132)

Chicken with Oranges—II

American

Topped with orange segments, this is a visually appealing dish with a fresh and lively taste.

You will need ...

Preparation ...

Assemble and prepare all ingredients.

2 Tbs butter
2 Tbs oil
Serving-pieces of chicken for 6 persons
Salt
Pepper

In casserole, heat butter and oil and brown chicken; season. Remove.

½ cup sherry
½ cup white wine

To casserole, add sherry and wine; over high heat, cook, stirring and scraping to deglaze casserole. Reduce heat to gentle.

Grated rind of 2 oranges
Grated rind of 1 lemon
Juice of oranges and lemon plus other orange juice to equal 1½ cups

To contents of casserole, add grated rinds and juice.

1 cup sour cream
3 Tbs flour

Mix sour cream with flour until smooth; add to casserole and, over high heat, cook, stirring, until sauce thickens.

At this point you may stop and continue later.

Cooking ...

Segments of 2 oranges, seeded and membranes removed *or* 1 orange, seeded and sliced paper thin

Replace chicken, spooning sauce over. Bake, covered, at 350° for 1 hour, or until chicken is tender. Arrange segments over contents of casserole for final 15 minutes of cooking.

Serve with ... Barley (p. 115)
Spinach Salad with sweet red pepper (p. 131)

Chicken with Oregano

Greek

A pungent chicken casserole.

You will need . . .	Preparation . . .
	Assemble and prepare all ingredients.
Juice of 4 lemons 1½ **tsp salt** 3 **Tbs (generous) dried oregano** **Serving-pieces of chicken for 6 persons**	Stir together lemon juice, salt, and oregano. In lightly oiled casserole, arrange chicken, skin side down; pour lemon juice mixture over. Bake, covered, at 350° for 30 minutes.
¼ **cup olive oil** **Pepper** 1 **28-oz. can Italian tomatoes**	Turn chicken pieces, sprinkle with olive oil, and season with pepper. Add tomatoes.
	At this point you may stop and continue later.

Cooking . . .

Bake, covered, at 350° for 30 minutes, or until chicken is tender.

Serve with . . . Bulgur (p. 115)
Green Salad with White Grapes (p. 128)

Chicken with Oysters

American

I cannot pretend to have a "favorite" among recipes in this book, but if obliged to name the ten most popular, this dish would be one.

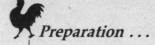

You will need . . .	*Preparation . . .*
	Assemble and prepare all ingredients.
. **Seasoned flour** **Serving-pieces of chicken** **for 6 persons** 2 **Tbs butter** 2 **Tbs oil**	In seasoned flour, dredge chicken. In casserole, heat butter and oil and brown chicken. Remove.
¾ **tsp turmeric *or* paprika (to** **add color)**	To pan juices, add remaining seasoned flour and turmeric. Cook gently 5 minutes.
1 **pint stewing oysters** **Chicken broth** 1 **cup heavy cream, scalded**	In saucepan, cook oysters in their juice until they just begin to curl at the edges; strain, reserving oysters and liquor. To oyster liquor, add chicken broth to equal 2 cups. Combine with cream. Stir liquids into seasoned flour mixture and, over medium heat, cook, stirring, until sauce thickens. At this point you may stop and continue later.

Cooking . . .

Replace chicken, spooning sauce over. Bake, covered, at 350° for 1 hour, or until chicken is tender.

Reserved oysters	Over contents of casserole, arrange reserved oysters and return to oven, covered, for 5 minutes to heat oysters through.

Serve with . . . Spinach (green) noodles (prepare as package directs)
Watercress Salad with parsley and red onion (p. 132)

Chicken with Paprika

Austrian

The quaintness of historic Salzburg, living quietly under its blanket of February snow, is more appealing at this season, I feel, than during the weeks of its celebrated Festival. In all seasons, however, the Hotel Goldener Hirsch, my source for this recipe, is Salzburg's finest hotel and one of the best kitchens in Austria.

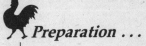

You will need ...	Preparation ...
	Assemble and prepare all ingredients.
2 Tbs butter 2 Tbs oil Serving-pieces of chicken for 6 persons Salt Pepper	In casserole, heat butter and oil and brown chicken; season. Remove.
3 onions, chopped 1 clove garlic, chopped	In remaining fat, cook onion and garlic until translucent.
2 Tbs paprika (preferably Hungarian) 2½ Tbs flour	Add paprika and flour and cook gently, stirring, for 3 minutes.
1 cup chicken broth 2 cups sour cream	Add broth and then sour cream, stirring constantly until sauce is smooth and thickened.
	At this point you may stop and continue later.

Cooking ...

Replace chicken. Bake, covered, at 350° for 1 hour, or until chicken is tender.

Serve with ... Noodles (p. 116) *or*
Potato Pancakes (p. 117)
Mixed Green Salad (p. 129)

Chicken with Peanut Sauce

Guinean

This recipe from West Africa is not recommended for the weight-watcher but it will win praise for the delicacy of its flavor.

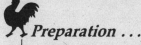

You will need ...	*Preparation ...*
	Assemble and prepare all ingredients.
2 **Tbs butter** 2 **Tbs oil** **Serving-pieces of chicken for 6 persons** **Salt** **Pepper**	In casserole, heat butter and oil and brown chicken; season. Remove.
2 **onions, chopped**	To fat in casserole, add onions and cook until translucent.
1 **1-lb. can Italian tomatoes, drained (reserve liquor)** 1 **9-oz. package frozen okra** 1 **large green pepper, chopped**	Add vegetables to onion, stirring to blend mixture. Replace chicken.
Reserved tomato liquor **Chicken broth *or* tomato juice *or* water** 1 **cup (1 8-oz. jar) smooth peanut butter** ½ **tsp salt** ¼ **tsp pepper** 1 **tsp sugar** ¼ **tsp fenugreek *or* cumin (optional)**	To reserved liquor from canned tomatoes, add one of the other suggested liquids to equal 1½ cups; add peanut butter and stir until mixture is smooth. Add seasonings, stir to blend mixture, and pour sauce over chicken. At this point you may stop and continue later.
	## Cooking ...
½ **cup peanuts, coarsely ground**	Bake, covered, at 350° for 1 hour, or until chicken is tender. When serving, garnish with ground peanuts.

Serve with ... Rice (p. 115)
Mixed Green Salad (p. 129)

Chicken with Pears

Middle Eastern   (Does not freeze)

In the Middle East, fruits are often used in combination with meats. In this country, we do so considerably less, but the loss is ours, for fruit and meat are unusually harmonious companions—as I believe this recipe will illustrate.

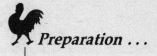

You will need ...	Preparation ...
	Assemble and prepare all ingredients.
2 Tbs butter 2 Tbs oil Serving-pieces of chicken for 6 persons Salt Pepper	In casserole, heat butter and oil and brown chicken; season. Remove. Discard all but 2 Tbs fat.
2 onions, chopped 1 tsp sugar 1 tsp cinnamon 1 tsp dried mint flakes, powdered	In remaining fat, cook onion until translucent. Replace chicken. Add seasonings. At this point you may stop and continue later.

Cooking ...

1 cup chicken broth	Over contents of casserole, pour broth; bake, covered, at 350° for 40 minutes.
3 firm pears, cut in lengthwise eighths Grated rind and juice of 1 lemon 2 Tbs brown sugar	Over chicken, arrange pears; sprinkle with lemon rind and juice; add brown sugar. Continue to bake, covered, for 20 minutes.

Serve with ... Rolls (p. 121)
Green Salad with White Grapes (p. 128)

Chicken with Pimento
Mexican

The preparation of this distinctive dish is simplified by the use of an electric blender in step 5; in the absence of a blender, the pimento may be pureed by forcing it through a sieve.

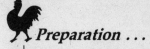

You will need ...   Preparation ...

Assemble and prepare all ingredients.

You will need ...	Preparation ...
2 **Tbs butter** 2 **Tbs oil** **Serving-pieces of chicken for 6 persons** **Salt** **Pepper**	In casserole, heat butter and oil and brown chicken; season. Remove.
2 **onions, chopped** 2 **cloves garlic, chopped**	In remaining fat, cook onion and garlic until translucent.
3 **Tbs flour**	Add flour and, over gentle heat, cook, stirring, for five minutes. Replace chicken.
2 **7-oz. cans pimento, with liquid** 1 **tsp salt** 1 **tsp sugar** 1 **tsp powdered cumin** **Juice and grated rind of 1 lemon** 1 **10-oz. can chicken broth**	In container of electric blender, combine these seven ingredients and blend on low speed until mixture is smooth (about 15 seconds). Add water to equal 2½ cups. Pour sauce over chicken. At this point you may stop and continue later.

Cooking ...

Bake, covered, at 350° for 1 hour, or until chicken is tender.

Serve with ... Corn Muffins (p. 122)
Green Bean Salad (p. 128) *or*
Lentils with Oil and Lemon (p. 129)

Chicken with Pineapple—I

Hawaiian

Delicate and fruity, a good warm weather dish.

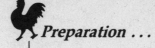

You will need ...

Preparation ...

Assemble and prepare all ingredients.

2	Tbs butter
2	Tbs oil
	Serving-pieces of chicken for 6 persons
	Salt
	Pepper

In casserole, heat butter and oil and brown chicken; season. Remove. Discard excess fat.

	Juice from a 20-oz. can pineapple chunks
1½	cups chicken broth
¼	cup soy sauce
¼	cup cider vinegar
3	Tbs cornstarch
2	Tbs sugar

In casserole, combine these four liquid ingredients. Combine cornstarch and sugar and stir into liquid mixture. Over high heat, cook, stirring constantly, until sauce thickens. Replace chicken.

At this point you may stop and continue later.

Cooking ...

Bake, covered, at 350° for 1 hour, or until chicken is tender.

¼	cup chopped preserved ginger (optional)
6	scallions, chopped (with as much green as possible)
1	green pepper, chopped
1	can water chestnuts, drained and sliced
	Reserved pineapple chunks
1½	cups grated coconut

To contents of casserole, add the first five ingredients; top with coconut and return to oven, uncovered, to heat through (about 10 minutes).

If desired, coconut may be toasted in oven before being added to casserole.

Serve with ... Rice (p. 115)
Mixed Green Salad (p. 129)

Chicken with Pineapple—II

Indochinese

In this delicate and aromatic dish, the specific flavors are elusive. (It may also be made with fish filets: simmer the sauce for 30 minutes; add filets, cut into bite-size pieces, top with pineapple, and cook, covered, for 10 minutes longer; serve in soup bowls over rice.)

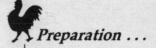

You will need ...

Preparation ...

	Assemble and prepare all ingredients.
2 **Tbs butter** 2 **Tbs oil** **Serving-pieces of chicken for 6 persons** **Salt** **Pepper**	In casserole, heat butter and oil and brown chicken; season. Remove.
2 **onions, chopped** 2 **cloves garlic, chopped**	Discard all but 2 Tbs fat; add onion and garlic and cook until translucent.
2 **Tbs soy sauce** ⅓ **cup sherry** **Juice from a 20-oz. can crushed pineapple (reserve fruit)**	Combine these liquids, add to onion and garlic, and deglaze casserole.
Grated rind and juice of 1 lemon 2 **bay leaves** 6 **corns whole allspice** 1 **tsp cumin seed** 1 **tsp cracked ginger root (optional)** ½ **tsp dried mint, crumbled** ½ **tsp red pepper flakes** ¼ **tsp saffron, crumbled**	To contents of casserole, add these nine ingredients.

continued ...

¼ cup cold water
4 Tbs cornstarch
3 cups boiling water

Mix water and cornstarch and add to casserole; immediately add boiling water and cook, stirring, until mixture thickens.

At this point you may stop and continue later.

Cooking ...

Reserved crushed pineapple
Shredded coconut (optional)

Replace chicken, and cover with sauce; bake, covered, at 350° for 1 hour, or until chicken is tender. Top with pineapple and coconut and heat through.

Serve with ... Rice (in soup bowls) (p. 115)
Oriental Salad (p. 130)

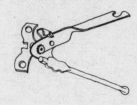

Chicken with Pineapple—III

Mexican

Raisins and cinnamon are distinctive in this dish.

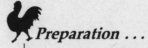

You will need . . .	**Preparation . . .**
	Assemble and prepare all ingredients.
Seasoned flour Serving-pieces of chicken for 6 persons 2 Tbs butter 2 Tbs oil	In seasoned flour, dredge chicken. In casserole, heat butter and oil and brown chicken. Sprinkle with 2 Tbs remaining seasoned flour.
1 cup orange juice 1 cup white wine 2 Tbs sugar 1 tsp cinnamon ½ tsp ground clove	Combine these five ingredients, blend well, and pour over chicken.
½ cup seedless raisins 1 8-oz. can crushed pineapple	Over contents of casserole, arrange a layer of raisins, then of pineapple. At this point you may stop and continue later.
	### Cooking . . .
½ cup toasted slivered almonds	Bake, covered, at 350° for 1 hour, or until chicken is tender. Before serving, top with sprinkling of almonds.

Serve with . . . Barley (p. 115)
Cucumber Salad (p. 127)

Chicken with Pineapple Juice

American

For those who want the flavor of pineapple without the presence of the fruit itself.

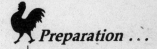

You will need ...	**Preparation ...**
	Assemble and prepare all ingredients.
Seasoned flour **Serving-pieces of chicken** **for 6 persons** 2 **Tbs butter** 2 **Tbs oil**	In seasoned flour, dredge chicken. In casserole, heat butter and oil and brown chicken. Remove.
2 **onions, chopped** 1 **clove garlic, chopped**	In remaining fat, cook onion and garlic until translucent.
2 **cups pineapple juice**	To contents of casserole, add pineapple juice and, over high heat, cook vigorously to deglaze casserole.
½ **tsp cinnamon** ½ **tsp ground allspice** ½ **tsp ginger (optional)**	Stir in spices; replace chicken.
	At this point you may stop and continue later.
	Cooking ...
	Bake, covered, at 350° for 1 hour, or until chicken is tender.

Serve with ... Rice (p. 115)
                 Spinach Salad with mushrooms (p. 131)

Chicken with Plum Sauce
Malayan

The tart-sweet sauce is complemented by the sweet cashews.

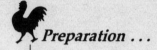

You will need ...   ## Preparation ...

Assemble and prepare all ingredients.

2	Tbs butter
2	Tbs oil

In casserole, heat butter and oil and brown chicken; season. Remove.

Serving-pieces of chicken for 6 persons
Salt
Pepper

1   cup tart plum jam
2   Tbs cornstarch
2   Tbs preserved ginger, chopped
1   clove garlic, minced
2   Tbs soy sauce
2   Tbs sherry
2   Tbs cider vinegar
1½ cups chicken broth

In casserole, removed from heat and somewhat cooled, combine jam and cornstarch, stirring until mixture is smooth. Add ginger, garlic, and liquid ingredients and, over high heat, cook, stirring, until sauce thickens. Replace chicken, spooning sauce over.

At this point you may stop and continue later.

Cooking ...

Bake, covered, at 350° for 1 hour, or until chicken is tender.

½   cup oven-roasted cashews, coarsely broken

When serving, sprinkle cashews over.

Serve with ... Rice (p. 115)
Oriental Salad (p. 130)

Chicken with Pork

Filipino

Grandmother Boucher, who produced the recipes for Chicken with Dumplings and Rolls, also produced a son who, with his young bride, went off to teach in the Philippines just prior to World War II. Returning home before the events at Pearl Harbor, they managed to reach America by an eastward route: China, India, the Middle East, and Europe. Among their chattels was a new-born son and this recipe for Chicken with Pork.

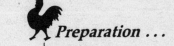

You will need ...

Preparation ...

Assemble and prepare all ingredients.

2	Tbs butter
2	Tbs oil
12	serving-pieces of chicken
2	lbs. lean pork, cubed

In casserole, heat butter and oil and brown chicken. Remove. In remaining fat, brown pork; over gentle heat, cook, covered, for 30 minutes, turning occasionally. Remove.

1	cup chicken broth
⅓	cup cider vinegar
⅓	cup sherry
⅓	cup soy sauce, *mixed with*
2	Tbs cornstarch
3	cloves garlic
½	tsp pepper
1	*or* 2 chicken livers, sieved (optional)

Combine liquids; add cornstarch and garlic, put through press; add pepper and liver. In casserole, cook over high heat, stirring, until sauce thickens. Replace chicken and pork, spooning sauce over.

At this point you may stop and continue later.

Cooking ...

Bake, covered, at 350° for 1 hour, or until chicken and pork are tender.

Serve with ... Rice (p. 115)
Oriental Salad (p. 130)

Chicken with Prunes
German

One would not expect the flavors of chicken and prunes to complement each other, but they do—deliciously.

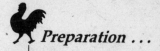

You will need ...   ## Preparation ...

Assemble and prepare all ingredients.

2	Tbs butter
2	Tbs oil
	Serving-pieces of chicken for 6 persons
	Salt
	Pepper

In casserole, heat butter and oil and brown chicken; season. Remove.

2	carrots, sliced thin
1	onion, chopped

In remaining fat, cook carrots and onion, stirring to coat well, until onion is translucent. Replace chicken.

1	lb. pitted prunes
	Juice of 1 lemon

To contents of casserole, add prunes and lemon juice.

At this point you may stop and continue later.

Cooking ...

1½	cups chicken broth
1	Tbs cornstarch

In saucepan, mix broth and cornstarch; cook, stirring, until sauce thickens. Pour over contents of casserole. Bake, covered, at 350° for 1 hour, or until chicken is tender.

Serve with ... Potato Pancakes (p. 117)
Cucumber Salad (p. 127)

Chicken with Red Cabbage

Polish

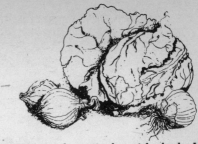

Flavorful and colorful, this dish is often made natively with duck; I prefer it made with chicken, however, for it is lighter and less rich.

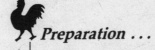

You will need ...

Preparation ...

Assemble and prepare all ingredients.

1	**medium red cabbage, shredded** **Boiling water**

Over cabbage, pour boiling water to cover; drain.

¼	**lb. salt pork, diced** **Serving-pieces of chicken for 6 persons** **Salt** **Pepper**

In casserole, render salt pork until crisp; remove to absorbent paper and reserve. In remaining fat, brown chicken; season. Remove. Discard all but 3 Tbs pan juices.

2	**onions, chopped**
2	**Tbs flour**

In pan juices, cook onion until translucent. Add flour and, over gentle heat, cook, stirring, for 5 minutes.

1	**cup red wine**
1	**tsp salt**
¼	**tsp pepper**
1½	**tsp sugar**
1	**tsp caraway seed**

Add wine and cook, stirring, until sauce thickens. Stir in seasonings and then cabbage.

At this point you may stop and continue later.

Cooking ...

Bake cabbage, covered, at 350° for 15 or 20 minutes. Replace chicken, spooning cabbage mixture over. Bake, covered, at 350° for 1 hour, or until chicken is tender.

Serve with ... Potato Pancakes (p. 117)
Mixed Green Salad (p. 129)

Chicken with Red Wine—I

American

This dish may be derived from the French classic that follows on the next page. Of the two, the French recipe is much superior, but the American is quicker to prepare.

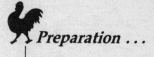

You will need ...	Preparation ...
	Assemble and prepare all ingredients.

2   Tbs butter
2   Tbs oil
      Serving-pieces of chicken
            for 6 persons
      Salt
      Pepper
	In casserole, heat butter and oil and brown chicken; season. Remove.

2 Tbs flour	To remaining fat, add flour; over gentle heat, cook, stirring, for about 5 minutes.
1½ cups red wine ¼ cup soy sauce 1 clove garlic, pressed 1 tsp ginger ½ tsp oregano 2 Tbs brown sugar	Combine these six ingredients and add gradually to flour mixture, stirring. Over high heat, cook, stirring, until sauce thickens. Replace chicken. At this point you may stop and continue later. ## Cooking ... Bake, covered, at 350° for 1 hour, or until chicken is tender.

Serve with ... Barley (p. 115)
Green Salad with White Grapes (p. 128)

Chicken with Red Wine—II

French

The classic *coq au vin* from France is really a *poulet bourguignonne*, distin-
continued ...

guishing it from its cousin *boeuf bourguignonne.* For information on the source of this recipe, see Chicken with Mustard Sauce.

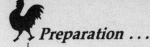

You will need ...	**Preparation ...**
	Assemble and prepare all ingredients.
¼ lb. salt pork, diced	In casserole, render pork bits; remove to absorbent paper and reserve.
12 to 18 small onions, peeled 6 carrots, cut in ½-inch pieces ½ lb. mushrooms, quartered	In fat, glaze onions, then carrots; remove and reserve. To remaining fat, add mushrooms, stirring to coat well; remove and reserve.
Serving-pieces of chicken for 6 persons	In remaining fat, brown chicken (butter may be added if necessary).
½ cup cognac	Warm cognac, ignite, and pour over chicken.
1½ tsp salt 1 tsp sugar ½ tsp pepper 3 Tbs parsley, minced ¼ tsp ground allspice 1 bay leaf, broken ¼ tsp celery seed 2 tsp chervil *or* marjoram ½ tsp thyme	When cognac flame dies, sprinkle chicken with seasonings. Add reserved vegetables and top with pork bits.
	At this point you may stop and continue later.

Cooking ...

½ cup beef bouillon 3 Tbs tarragon vinegar 5 Tbs flour	In container with tight-fitting lid, combine bouillon, vinegar, and flour; shake until mixture is smooth and pour over contents of casserole.
Dry red wine	Add wine just to cover. Bake, covered, at 350° for 1 hour, or until chicken is tender. If sauce seems thin, remove lid and bake 15 minutes longer.
	If desired, ¼ lb. thick-sliced bacon, diced, may be substituted for salt pork.

Serve with ... French Bread (p. 120)
Mixed Green Salad (p. 129)

Chicken with Rice—I

American

This dish is my concoction and is easily prepared well in advance.

You will need ...

Preparation ...

Assemble and prepare all ingredients.

2	Tbs butter
2	Tbs oil
	Serving-pieces of chicken for 6 persons
	Salt
	Pepper

In casserole, heat butter and oil and brown chicken; season. Remove.

2	onions, chopped
2	cloves garlic, chopped
1	green pepper, chopped

In remaining fat, cook these three ingredients until translucent.

1½ cups natural raw rice

To contents of casserole, add rice, stirring to coat well.

1½	tsp curry powder
¾	tsp thyme
1	tsp salt
¼	tsp pepper
1	tsp sugar
½	cup seedless raisins *or* currants
1	28-oz. can Italian tomatoes, with juice

To rice mixture, add seasonings and raisins, stirring to blend well. Add tomatoes and stir to blend. Replace chicken, spooning rice mixture over.

At this point you may stop and continue later.

Cooking ...

Bake, covered, at 350° for 1 hour, or until chicken is tender and liquid is absorbed. (Check occasionally that there is enough liquid; add chicken broth if necessary.)

Serve with ... Mushrooms with Herbs (p. 130)
or Mixed Green Salad (p. 129)

Chicken with Rice—II

Dominican

Here is an ideal one-dish meal for hot weather, especially since its taste is as fresh as spring.

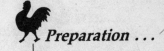

You will need ...	Preparation ...
	Assemble and prepare all ingredients.
2 **Tbs butter** 2 **Tbs oil** **Serving-pieces of chicken for 6 persons** **Salt** **Pepper**	In casserole, heat butter and oil and brown chicken; season. Remove.
1 **onion, chopped** 1 **clove garlic, chopped**	In remaining fat, cook onion and garlic until translucent.
1½ **cups natural raw rice** ¾ **tsp turmeric (optional)** ½ **lb. mushrooms, sliced (optional)**	Add rice, stirring to coat each grain; add turmeric, stirring to blend color evenly. Add mushrooms and cook over gentle heat, stirring occasionally, for 5 minutes. Replace chicken.
Grated rind and juice of 3 limes 1½ **tsp Angostura bitters** 1½ **Tbs brown sugar** 1 **tsp salt** **Chicken broth or water**	Combine lime rind, juice, bitters, sugar, and salt; add liquid to equal 3 cups. At this point you may stop and continue later.

Cooking ...

Over contents of casserole, pour liquid mixture; bake, covered, at 350° for 1 hour, or until chicken is tender and liquid is absorbed.

Serve with ... Mixed Green Salad (p. 129)

Chicken with Rice—III
Dutch

More accurately, this is a Dutch East Indian dish, called natively *nasi goreng,* but it is to be found in several restaurants throughout the Netherlands specializing in food from the Dutch dominions.

You will need . . . 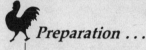 *Preparation* . . .

		Assemble and prepare all ingredients.
2	Tbs butter	In casserole, heat butter and oil and brown chicken; season. Remove.
2	Tbs oil	
12	serving-pieces of chicken for 6 persons	
	Salt	
	Pepper	
2	onions, chopped	In remaining fat, cook onion and celery until onion is translucent.
2	stalks celery, with tops, minced	
1½	cups natural raw rice	To contents of casserole, add rice, stirring to coat well with pan juices. Add seasonings, stirring. Replace chicken and add ham, spooning rice over.
2	cloves garlic, minced	
1	tsp coriander	
1	tsp cumin	
½	tsp mace	
½	tsp red pepper flakes	
1½	tsp salt	At this point you may stop and continue later.
1	tsp sugar	
1	4-oz. package boiled ham, cut in 2" julienne	

Cooking . . .

3	cups chicken broth	Over contents of casserole, pour chicken broth. Bake, covered, at 350° for 1 hour, or until chicken and rice are tender and liquid is absorbed. Add shrimp and continue to cook, covered, for 15 minutes.
1	lb. shrimp, shelled and deveined	

continued . . .

Coarsely chopped peanuts Soy sauce	If desired, serve with side dish of peanuts for garnish and soy sauce for added flavor.

Serve with ... Oriental Salad (p. 130)

Chicken with Rice—IV

Middle Eastern

Although I do not know for certain the nationality of this recipe, a Middle Eastern origin is suggested by its use of fruit as a complement to meat cooked with rice.

You will need ... Preparation ...

Assemble and prepare all ingredients.

2 Tbs butter 2 Tbs oil Serving-pieces of chicken for 6 persons Salt Pepper	In casserole, heat butter and oil and brown chicken; season. Remove.
2 onions, chopped 1½ cups natural raw rice 24 tenderized dried apricots, quartered	In remaining fat, cook onion until translucent. Add rice, stirring to coat well. Add apricots, stirring to coat well. Replace chicken, spooning rice mixture over.
1½ cups chicken broth 1½ cups red wine 1 tsp salt ½ tsp pepper	Combine broth, wine, and seasonings. Pour over. At this point you may stop and continue later.

Cooking ...

Bake, covered, at 350° for 1 hour, or until chicken and rice are tender and liquid is absorbed.

Serve with ... Spinach Salad with mushrooms (p. 131)

Chicken with Rice—V

Arabian

Cardamon is the distinctive flavor in this one-dish meal.

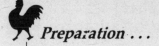

You will need ...   **Preparation ...**

Assemble and prepare all ingredients.

2	Tbs butter
2	Tbs oil
	Serving-pieces of chicken for 6 persons

In casserole, heat butter and oil and brown chicken. Remove.

| 3 | onions, sliced |
| 3 | carrots, coarsely grated |

Cook onion and carrot until onion is translucent.

1½	cups natural raw rice
1½	tsp ground cardamon
½	tsp ground cinnamon
½	tsp ground clove
1	tsp salt
½	tsp pepper
1	tsp sugar

Add rice and seasonings, stirring to blend mixture.

Replace chicken, covering with rice mixture.

At this point you may stop and continue later.

Cooking ...

| 1½ | cups chicken broth |
| 1½ | cups tomato juice |

In sauce pan, combine liquids and bring to the boil; pour over contents of casserole. Bake, covered, at 350° for 1 hour, or until chicken is tender.

Serve with ... Cucumber Salad (p. 127)

Chicken with Rice—VI

Pakistani

The recipe may be made with either rice (I prefer brown) or bulgur. If fresh ginger root is unavailable, preserved ginger will substitute (in this case, omit the sugar).

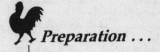

You will need ...

Preparation ...

Assemble and prepare all ingredients.

2	**Tbs butter**
2	**Tbs oil**
	Serving-pieces of chicken for 6 persons
	Salt
	Pepper

In casserole, heat butter and oil, brown chicken; season. Remove.

3   **onions, chopped**

In remaining fat, cook onion until translucent.

1½ **cups natural raw rice**

Add rice, stirring until each grain is coated.

	Juice of 1 lemon
2	**tsp salt**
¼	**tsp pepper**
1	**tsp sugar**
¾	**tsp ginger**
1	**Tbs chopped fresh ginger root (or more, to taste)**

Into rice-onion mixture, stir seasonings. Replace chicken, spooning rice around and over it.

At this point you may stop and continue later.

Cooking ...

2	**cups yogurt**
1	**cup chicken broth**

Combine yogurt and broth, pour over contents of casserole; bake, covered, at 350° for 1 hour, or until chicken is tender and liquid is absorbed.

Serve with ... Salad of your choice

Chicken with Rice—VII

Spanish

Paella Valenciana is made with seafood only; this recipe derives from the preceding one, *arroz con pollo,* and from the well-known paella. The combination of chicken and seafood with seasoning ingredients is delectable. The dish is particularly suitable for party fare.

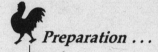

You will need ...	*Preparation ...*
	Assemble and prepare all ingredients.
¼ cup olive oil Serving-pieces of chicken for 6 persons Salt Pepper	In casserole, heat oil and brown chicken; season. Remove.
¼ lb. salt pork, diced	In remaining oil, render salt pork until crisp; remove and reserve. Discard all but 3 Tbs fat.
2 onions, chopped 1 clove garlic, chopped	In reserved fat, cook onion and garlic until translucent.
1½ cups natural raw rice ½ tsp saffron ½ tsp turmeric	Add rice, stirring to coat well. Add seasonings, stirring to blend mixture.
1 lb. raw shrimp, shelled and deveined 12 Littleneck clams in shell (optional) Several thin slices of chorizo *or* other hard sausage 2 20-oz. cans Italian tomatoes, drained (reserve liquid)	To rice, add reserved chicken, shrimp, clams, sausage, and tomatoes.

Reserved tomato liquid
½ cup white wine
¼ cup cognac
1 cup clam juice
  Chicken broth, as needed
1 tsp salt

Combine liquids to equal three cups; add salt and dissolve.

At this point you may stop and continue later.

Cooking ...

½ cup pitted green olives, halved

Over contents of casserole, pour liquid mixture. Sprinkle with reserved pork bits and olives. Bake, covered, at 350° for 1 hour, or until chicken and rice are tender and liquid is absorbed. The dish should be moist; neither liquid nor dry.

Serve with ... Spinach Salad with sweet red pepper (p. 131)

Chicken with Rice—VIII
Spanish

Arroz con pollo is as Spanish as castanets. Served with a generous salad, it makes a substantial one-dish meal. The variation given below is for a simplified paella, another national dish in Spain.

You will need ...    Preparation ...

2 **Tbs butter** 2 **Tbs oil** **Serving-pieces of chicken for 6 persons** **Salt** **Pepper**	Assemble and prepare all ingredients. In casserole, heat butter and oil and brown chicken; season. Remove.
1 **onion, chopped** 1 **clove garlic, chopped,** 1 **green pepper, chopped**	To remaining fat in casserole, add onion, garlic, and pepper; cook until translucent.
1½ **cups natural raw rice** **Saffron (a generous pinch)**	Add rice and cook, stirring, until grains are well coated. Add saffron, crumbling it between the fingers; stir to blend mixture. Replace chicken. At this point you may stop and continue later.

Cooking ...

3 **cups hot chicken broth**	Over contents of casserole, pour broth. Bake, covered, at 350° for 1 hour, or until chicken is tender and liquid is absorbed. *Variation:* for a simplified paella, follow steps #1 through #4, adding ½ tsp dill and the grated rind of 1 lemon; stir in 1 lb. raw or frozen shrimp; replace chicken. Combine juice of 1 lemon, 1 cup dry white wine, and chicken broth to equal 3 cups; proceed with step #5; add ½ cup frozen peas after first 45 minutes and garnish with 2 canned pimentos, chopped.

Serve with ... Mixed Green Salad (p. 129)

Chicken with Ripe Olives

Italian

One of the most satisfying chicken dishes I know—its aroma always evokes memories of my first trip to Florence and the Pitti Palace!

You will need ...

Preparation ...

Assemble and prepare all ingredients.

	Seasoned flour
	Serving-pieces of chicken for 6 persons
4	Tbs olive oil
1	clove garlic, split

In seasoned flour, dredge chicken. In casserole, heat oil and cook garlic until slightly golden; discard. Brown chicken (a little oil may be added as necessary).

⅓ cup cognac

Warm cognac, ignite, and pour over.

1	bay leaf, broken
3	Tbs parsley, chopped
1	tsp sage
½	tsp thyme
¾	tsp salt
1	1-lb. can Italian tomatoes

Over chicken, distribute seasonings. Pour over tomatoes.

¾ cup white wine

Mix wine with 1 Tbs remaining seasoned flour until smooth. Pour over contents of casserole.

At this point you may stop and continue later.

Cooking ...

1 cup pitted ripe olives, quartered lengthwise

Bake, covered, at 350° for 1 hour, or until chicken is tender. At end of first 30 minutes, sprinkle olives over.

Serve with ... Spaghetti (p. 116)
Mixed Green Salad (p. 129)

Chicken with Sauerkraut

Alsatian

The cousin of Chicken with Red Cabbage, but a heartier dish, I feel, and perhaps a bit easier to make.

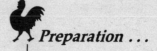

You will need ...	*Preparation ...*
	Assemble and prepare all ingredients.
2 Tbs butter	In casserole, heat butter and oil and brown chicken; season. Remove.
2 Tbs oil	
Serving-pieces of chicken for 6 persons	
Salt	
Pepper	
1 onion, chopped	In remaining fat, cook onion and apple until onion is translucent.
1 tart apple, peeled, cored, and diced	
1 tsp caraway seed (optional)	To onion mixture, add caraway seed and sugar, stirring to blend mixture. Add sauerkraut and cornstarch. Toss well. Replace chicken.
1 Tbs brown sugar	
1 2-lb. can sauerkraut, rinsed and well drained	
1 Tbs cornstarch, *mixed with* 3 Tbs water	
	At this point you may stop and continue later.

Cooking ...

Bake, covered, at 350° for 1 hour, or until chicken is tender.

Serve with ... Potato Pancakes (p. 117)
or
Hominy (p. 118)
or
Beans in Garlic Oil (p. 127)

Chicken with Shrimp

Italian

One of my favorite recipes for doubling; it does so very easily. The sauce is tasty with rice or spaghetti, and the flavors of chicken and shrimp complement each other nicely.

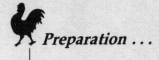

You will need ...

Preparation ...

Assemble and prepare all ingredients.

2	Tbs butter
2	Tbs oil
12	serving-pieces of chicken
	Salt
	Pepper

In casserole, heat butter and oil and brown chicken; season. Remove.

3	onions, chopped
2	cloves garlic, chopped
2	Tbs flour

In remaining fat, cook onion and garlic until translucent. Add flour, stirring to blend the mixture well.

1	1-lb. can tomato sauce
1	cup red wine
2	tsp each: basil, oregano
3	Tbs minced parsley
1	tsp salt
¼	tsp pepper
1	tsp sugar

To contents of casserole, add tomato sauce, wine, and seasonings; cook, stirring, until sauce thickens somewhat. Replace chicken and spoon sauce over.

At this point you may stop and continue later.

Cooking ...

1 lb. raw shrimp, shelled and deveined (frozen raw shrimp, fully thawed, may be used)

Bake, covered, at 350° for 1 hour, or until chicken is tender. Add shrimp and continue to cook, covered, at 350° for 15 minutes, or until shrimp turn pink.

Serve with ... Rice (p. 115)
or
Spaghetti (p. 116)
Green Bean Salad with cherry tomatoes (p. 128)

Chicken with Soup

Necessity was the mother of this invention (I cannot dignify it with the term "recipe"). I suddenly realized that for a friend's Metropolitan Opera debut I had done nothing for an after-theater celebration. The chicken was already browned (but frozen) and the soup was on the shelf. Midnight supper consisted of this menu.

You will need ... *Preparation ...*

Assemble and prepare all ingredients.

2   **Tbs butter**
2   **Tbs oil**
   **Serving-pieces of chicken
     for 6 persons**
   Salt
   Pepper

In casserole, heat butter and oil and brown chicken; season.

2   **onions, chopped (optional)**
1   **clove garlic, chopped (optional)**

If onions and garlic are used, remove chicken and cook onion and garlic until translucent. Replace chicken.

At this point you may stop and continue later.

1   **can cream of mushroom
    soup, undiluted**
½   **cup milk**
   Grated rind of 1 lemon
1   **tsp ground cumin**

Combine soup, milk, and seasonings; pour over contents of casserole.

Cooking ...

Bake, covered, at 350° for 1 hour, or until chicken is tender.

The following herbs and seasonings can be used: ½ to ¾ tsp powdered allspice, basil, chili powder, coriander, ginger, marjoram, nutmeg, oregano, rosemary, sage, savory, tarragon, or thyme; and, of course, bay leaf.

The following cream- or bisque-type soups can be used: asparagus, celery (add ½ cup chopped fresh celery), cheddar cheese, chicken, corn, pea, potato, shrimp, spinach, tomato; adjust consistency of sauce by amount of milk added.

Serve with ... Rice (p. 115)
                 Mixed Green Salad (p. 129)

Chicken with Sour Cream

Bulgarian

The irrepressible Ljuba Welitsch's three glorious seasons as *prima donna assoluta* (1948–51) at the Metropolitan Opera crowned a career already acclaimed in Europe. A woman of ebullient enthusiasm, good humor, and passionate feelings about everyone and everything, she now has a career in European motion pictures and television. She might, if she wanted, have a career as a cook—as the following recipe will attest. The English transliteration of her name, "Great Love," *is* Ljuba: bigger than life and twice the fun. This recipe was sung out from the kitchen as she prepared it; I have adapted it to American products and quantities.

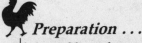

You will need . . .

2	**Tbs butter**
2	**Tbs oil**
1	**clove garlic, sliced length-** **wise**
	Serving-pieces of chicken **for 6 persons**
	Salt
	Pepper

3	**Tbs flour**
2	**cups sour cream**

18	**mushrooms, quartered**
3	**Tbs parsley, minced**
1	**Tbs dried dillweed**
1	**tsp powdered cumin**
3	**scallions, minced (with as** **much green as possi-** **ble)**
	Grated rind and juice of 1 **lemon**

Preparation . . .

Assemble and prepare all ingredients.

In casserole, heat butter and oil and cook garlic until fat is flavored; discard garlic. Brown chicken; season. Remove.

To pan juices, add flour, stirring to blend mixture. Add sour cream and, over gentle heat, cook, stirring constantly, for a few minutes.

To sour cream mixture, add these seven ingredients; stir to blend mixture.

At this point you may stop and continue later.

Cooking . . .

Replace chicken. Bake, covered, at 350° for 1 hour, or until chicken is tender.

Serve with . . . Rice (p. 115) *or*
Noodles (p. 116)
Salad of your choice

Chicken with Spinach

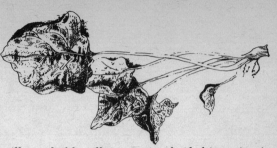

Italian

A 6-quart casserole will not hold sufficient spinach if this recipe is doubled. The dish does not freeze well. However, its best quality is its freshness.

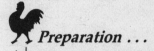

You will need ...

Preparation ...

Assemble and prepare all ingredients.

You will need ...	Preparation ...
Seasoned flour Serving-pieces of chicken for 6 persons 2 Tbs butter 2 Tbs oil	In seasoned flour, dredge chicken. In casserole, heat butter and oil and brown chicken. Remove. Pour off pan juices; reserve.
2 cups sour cream ½ cup heavy cream ¼ cup sherry Remaining seasoned flour 1 onion, coarsely chopped 1 clove garlic, chopped	In blender, combine these six ingredients and, on low speed, blend until smooth (about 15 seconds).
2 10-oz. packages fresh spinach, washed and well drained	Toss spinach with sour cream mixture; place in casserole and arrange chicken over; pour all reserved pan juices over. At this point you may stop and continue later.

Cooking ...

Bake, covered, at 350° for 1 hour, or until chicken is tender.

Serve with ... Noodles (p. 116)
Green Bean Salad (p. 128)

Chicken Stroganov

Chicken in stroganov sauce is as tasty as its more famous cousin, beef stroganov—and far less costly! Ideal for supper parties.

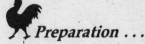

You will need ...

Preparation ...

Assemble and prepare all ingredients.

2 **Tbs butter**	In casserole, heat butter and oil and brown chicken; season. Remove.
2 **Tbs oil**	
Serving-pieces of chicken for 6 persons	
Salt	
Pepper	

3 **onions, chopped**
2 **cloves garlic, sliced lengthwise**

In remaining fat, cook onion and garlic until translucent. Remove and discard garlic.

4 **Tbs flour**
½ **tsp salt**
¼ **tsp white pepper**
1 **lb. mushrooms, sliced**

Into onion, stir flour, salt, and pepper; add mushrooms, cover, and cook for 5 minutes.

1 **can cream of mushroom soup**
2 **cups sour cream**

Stir in soup and simmer, covered, for 10 minutes. Add sour cream, stirring to blend mixture. Replace chicken.

At this point you may stop and continue later.

Cooking ...

Bake, covered, at 350° for 1 hour, or until chicken is tender.

Serve with ... Noodles (p. 116)
Watercress Salad with red onion (p. 132)

Chicken with Sweet-and-Sour Sauce
Chinese

Although using western cooking methods, this recipe tastes like fine Chinese cuisine.

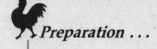

You will need ... | Preparation ...

Assemble and prepare all ingredients.

| Seasoned flour
| Serving-pieces of chicken for 6 persons
| 2 Tbs butter
| 2 Tbs oil

In seasoned flour, dredge chicken. In casserole, heat butter and oil and brown chicken.

2 onions, sliced
Juice from 20-oz. can pineapple tidbits

Add onion slices and pour juice over; simmer, covered, for 15 minutes.

At this point you may stop and continue later.

⅓ cup each: soy sauce, cider vinegar, water
4 Tbs honey

Combine liquids and honey and pour over contents of casserole.

Cooking ...

Bake, covered, at 350° for 30 minutes.

Reserved pineapple tidbits
2 green peppers, seeded and cut in chunks

To contents of casserole, add pineapple and pepper and continue to cook, covered, at 350° for 15 minutes, or until chicken is tender.

Serve with ... Rice (p. 115)
Oriental Salad (p. 130)

Chicken with Sweet Wine

You have a choice of wines, and therefore also nationalities: sherry or Madeira yield a Spanish dish; marsala an Italian one.

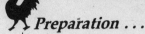

You will need ...	*Preparation ...*
	Assemble and prepare all ingredients.
Sweet wine of your choice **Water** **Serving-pieces of chicken for 6 persons**	In equal parts wine and water to cover, marinate chicken for about 6 hours. Drain and dry chicken; discard marinade.
2 Tbs butter **2 Tbs oil** **Salt** **Pepper**	In casserole, heat butter and oil and brown chicken; season. Remove.
1 onion, chopped **1 clove garlic, chopped**	In remaining fat, cook onion and garlic until translucent.
3 Tbs flour **1 tsp powdered cumin** **Grated rind of 1 orange**	To onion mixture, add flour and, over gentle heat, cook, stirring, for 5 minutes. Add seasonings, stirring to blend.
1 10-oz. can chicken broth **1 cup of sweet wine used in marinade** **Juice of 1 orange**	Combine liquids, add to contents of casserole and, over high heat, cook, stirring, until sauce thickens. Replace chicken, spooning sauce over.
	At this point you may stop and continue later.

Cooking ...

Bake, covered, at 350° for 1 hour, or until chicken is tender.

Serve with ... Barley (p. 115)
Spinach Salad with sweet red pepper (p. 131)

Chicken with Tapioca

American

When you announce the *pièce de résistance* as Chicken with Tapioca, no one will believe you. The tapioca disappears into one of the smoothest sauces imaginable.

You will need ...

Preparation ...

Assemble and prepare all ingredients.

2	Tbs butter
2	Tbs oil
	Serving-pieces of chicken for 6 persons
	Salt
	Pepper

In casserole, heat butter and oil and brown chicken; season. Remove.

2	cups celery, chopped
6	carrots, sliced
12	small onions
¼	lb. mushrooms, sliced (optional)

To fat in casserole, add vegetables. Stir and cook for 5 minutes.

⅓	cup instant tapioca
1½	tsp salt
½	tsp pepper
1	tsp sugar
1	tsp powdered allspice
½	cup chopped parsley
1	bay leaf
1	35-oz. can whole Italian tomatoes

Add tapioca, seasonings, and tomatoes; stir to blend mixture. Replace chicken.

At this point you may stop and continue later.

Cooking ...

Bake, covered, at 350° for 1 hour, or until chicken is tender.

Serve with ... Rolls (p. 121)
Spinach Salad with watercress (p. 131)

Chicken with Fresh Tarragon

French

I first enjoyed this delicate dish on the garden terrace of Antoinette Schulte's apartment overlooking Paris. Like the paintings of this esteemed American artist, Miss Schulte's cooking is fine and subtle. Accompanied by her stimulating conversation and that of her artist friends, a meal at her home is a memorable experience. In France, Miss Schulte makes this dish with a *petit suisse* cheese, similar to our cream cheese but not readily available in America.

You will need ...

Preparation ...

Assemble and prepare all ingredients.

¼ lb. salt pork, diced

In casserole, render salt pork until crisp; remove to absorbent paper and reserve.

Serving-pieces of chicken
for 6 persons
Salt
Pepper

In remaining fat, brown chicken; season. Remove. Discard all but 3 Tbs fat.

½ lb. mushrooms. sliced

In fat, sauté mushrooms for 5 minutes.

½ cup toasted slivered almonds (optional)

Replace chicken; sprinkle almonds and reserved pork bits over.

½ cup fresh tarragon leaves
2 8-oz. packages cream
cheese, at room
temperature
1 cup dry white wine
½ tsp salt
¼ tsp white pepper

Rinse, dry, and chop tarragon. In container of electric blender, combine cheese, wine, salt, and pepper; blend on low speed for 15 seconds. Add tarragon and immediately turn off blender.

At this point you may stop and continue later.

Cooking ...

Over contents of casserole, pour sauce; bake, covered, at 350° for 1 hour, or until chicken is tender.

Serve with ... New Potatoes (p. 117) *or*
Green Noodles (prepare as package directs)
Green Salad with White Grapes (p. 128)

Variations:

1) For curry-flavored sauce evocative of India: to cream cheese-wine mixture, add 1 generous Tbs curry powder.

2) For ginger-flavored sauce (perhaps my favorite, despite its lack of geographic origin): season chicken when browning with ½ tsp ground ginger, in addition to salt and pepper; to cream cheese-wine mixture, add another ½ tsp (generous) ground ginger; before pouring sauce over chicken, sprinkle contents of casserole with ¼ cup diced fresh ginger root (preserved will do) and 1 tsp sugar.

3) For mint-flavored sauce: to cream cheese-wine mixture, add ¼ cup fresh mint leaves, chopped.

Chicken with Tomatoes

French

Chicken *Marengo,* as this dish is often called, derives its name from one of Napoleon's victorious battles. Whether or not the Emperor ate chicken prepared this way at the time of his conquest, I cannot say— but it would have been a suitable dish for the occasion.

You will need ...

Preparation ...

Assemble and prepare all ingredients.

You will need ...	Preparation ...

2   Tbs butter
2   Tbs oil
     Serving-pieces of chicken
          for 6 persons
     Salt
     Pepper
	In casserole, heat butter and oil and brown chicken; season. Remove.

1 onion, chopped 2 cloves garlic, minced	In remaining fat, cook onion and garlic until translucent.
1 cup white wine 1 cup chicken broth 1 bay leaf 3 Tbs parsley, chopped ½ tsp tarragon ½ tsp thyme 1 tsp salt ¼ tsp pepper 1 tsp sugar	To contents of casserole, add liquids and seasonings and, over high heat, cook, uncovered, for 10 minutes.

3   ripe fresh tomatoes,
          peeled, seeded, and
          coarsely chopped
	Add tomatoes, stirring to blend sauce. Replace chicken.
	
	At this point you may stop and continue later.

Cooking ...

½ lb. mushrooms, sautéed	Bake, covered, at 350° for 1 hour, or until chicken is tender. Add mushrooms and continue to cook, covered, for 10 minutes, or until mushrooms are heated through.

Serve with ... New Potatoes (p. 117) *or* Barley (p. 115)
Spinach Salad with watercress (p. 131)

Chicken with Tomato Sauce

Flemish

One January evening in Amsterdam, I enjoyed the warm hospitality and good food of the Dorrius Restaurant, among the oldest and most interesting of that city. The Dorrius serves Dutch food in a Dutch setting; there is no pretense, no bid for tourists. Of several excellent meals there, none was more enjoyable than that which introduced me to this dish.

You will need ...	*Preparation ...*
	Assemble and prepare all ingredients.
2 Tbs butter 2 Tbs oil Serving-pieces of chicken for 6 persons Salt Pepper	In casserole, heat butter and oil and brown chicken; season. Remove.
1 onion, chopped	In remaining fat, cook onion until translucent.
3 Tbs flour 1 cup chicken broth 1 cup sour cream 1 1-lb can tomato puree Juice of ½ lemon ½ tsp celery seed 1 tsp sugar	Stir flour into onion; add chicken broth, stirring. When sauce starts to thicken add sour cream, puree, lemon juice and seasonings. Replace chicken.
	At this point you may stop and continue later.
	Cooking ...
Grated cheese	Bake, covered, at 350° for 1 hour, or until chicken is tender. Serve with sprinkling of grated cheese.

Serve with ... Noodles (p. 116)
Mushrooms with Herbs (p. 130)

Chicken with Vegetables—I

Alsatian

This recipe comes from Strasbourg, a city generous to a fault: it offers the traveler its remarkable cathedral, the fantasy of its fifteenth-century architecture, the delights of its many pâtés, and the picturesqueness of its Old City, where there are a number of first-rate restaurants. My favorite is the Restaurant Maison des Tanneurs where, on a spring day, I sat overlooking the canal and lunched on native pâté, chicken with vegetables, a local cheese, and *vin du pays*.

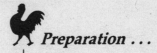

You will need . . .	*Preparation . . .*
	Assemble and prepare all ingredients.
2 **Tbs butter** 2 **Tbs oil** **Serving-pieces of chicken for 6 persons** **Salt** **Pepper**	In casserole, heat butter and oil and brown chicken; season. Remove.
3 **large *or* 6 small carrots, sliced thin** 3 **medium potatoes, peeled and sliced in lengthwise quarters**	In fat, stir carrots, coating well; remove and reserve. Repeat with potatoes.
3 **onions, chopped** 1 **clove garlic, chopped** ¼ **cup parsley, chopped**	In remaining fat, cook onions and garlic until translucent. Replace chicken and sprinkle with parsley.
1 **small cabbage, shredded** 1 **tsp salt** ½ **tsp pepper**	To contents of casserole, add carrots and cabbage; season.
	At this point you may stop and continue later. Store potatoes in airtight container.

continued . . .

Cooking ...

On top of stove, simmer gently, covered, for 15 minutes.

1   **cup white wine**
    Reserved potatoes

Pour wine over all; arrange potatoes on top. Bake, covered, at 350° for 1 hour.

Serve with ... French Bread (p. 120)

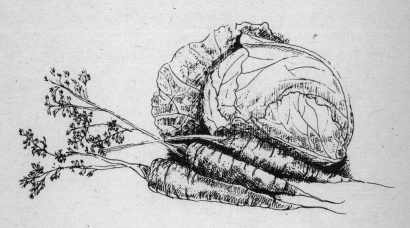

Chicken with Vegetables—II

Basque

This recipe provides a one-dish meal with a variety of vegetables and a strong regional flavor.

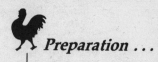

You will need ...

Preparation ...

Assemble and prepare all ingredients.

2	Tbs butter
2	Tbs oil
	Serving-pieces of chicken for 6 persons
	Salt
	Pepper

In casserole, heat butter and oil and brown chicken; season. Remove.

½	lb. mushrooms, quartered
1	small eggplant, diced
1	green pepper, chopped
3	tomatoes, peeled, seeded, and coarsely chopped
2	onions, sliced
2	cloves garlic, minced
¾	tsp basil
1	bay leaf
½	tsp thyme
2	tsp salt
1	tsp pepper
1	tsp sugar

In remaining fat, cook vegetables and seasonings, stirring, for 5 minutes; more oil may be added if necessary. Replace chicken, spooning vegetables over.

At this point you may stop and continue later.

Cooking ...

½ cup white wine

Over contents of casserole, pour wine; bake, covered, at 350° for 1 hour, or until chicken and vegetables are tender. More wine may be added if necessary; the dish should be moist but not liquid.

Serve with ... French Bread (p. 120)
Mixed Green Salad (p. 129)

Chicken with Vegetables—III

Chinese

Delicate and decorative, this is nearly a one-dish meal; and more vegetables may be used if desired. For example, 1 cup chopped celery cabbage or 1 package frozen pea pods or 1 can of bean sprouts, drained, may be added to the recipe for the final 15 minutes of cooking.

You will need . . . *Preparation . . .*

Assemble and prepare all ingredients.

2 Tbs butter
2 Tbs oil
  Serving-pieces of chicken for 6 persons
  Salt
  Pepper

In casserole, heat butter and oil and brown chicken; season. Remove. Discard excess fat.

¾ cup sherry
1 10-oz. can chicken broth
¼ cup soy sauce
3 Tbs cornstarch

In casserole, combine liquids and cornstarch and, over high heat, cook, stirring, until sauce thickens.

2 tsp ginger
1 Tbs sugar
2 Tbs preserved ginger, chopped (optional)

Add seasonings to sauce, stirring to blend well. Replace chicken.

At this point you may stop and continue later.

Cooking . . .

Bake, covered, at 350° for 45 minutes.

12 mushrooms, sliced
6 scallions, sliced (with as much green as possible)
1 can water chestnuts, sliced
1 green pepper, chopped
½ cup slivered almonds (optional)

Add vegetables and almonds and cook 15 minutes longer, or until chicken is tender.

Serve with . . . Rice (p. 115)
Oriental Salad (p. 130)

Chicken with Vegetables—IV

French

This dish is my adaptation of a fish stew called, in Basque, *aigo-sau*. The original is traditionally served in soup bowls, and I believe you will find its chicken cousin more enjoyable if served the same way. (Should you want to make the fish stew: follow this recipe, substituting ⅓ cup olive oil for the reserved chicken fat, water for the chicken broth, and add raw fish—2½ lbs. filet of cod or scrod cut in large bite-size pieces—for the final 15 minutes of cooking.)

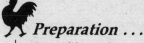

You will need . . .	*Preparation . . .*
	Assemble and prepare all ingredients.
2 **Tbs butter** 2 **Tbs oil** **Serving-pieces of chicken for 6 persons** **Salt** **Pepper**	In casserole, heat butter and oil and brown chicken; season. Remove. Pour off chicken fat and reserve.
4 **medium potatoes, peeled and cut in ⅛'s** 4 **medium onions, thickly sliced** 4 **carrots, scraped and cut in bite-size pieces** 4 **stalks celery, cut in bite-size pieces** 2 **green peppers, cut in lengthwise strips**	In casserole, arrange potatoes, onions, carrots, celery, and peppers in layers.
3 **cloves garlic, minced** 2 **tsp salt** ½ **tsp pepper** 2 **Tbs sugar** 2 **bay leaves, crushed** 1 **tsp oregano** 2 **Tbs parsley flakes** **Juice and grated rind of 1 orange** ⅓ **cup reserved chicken fat**	Over vegetables, distribute seasonings and chicken fat.

continued . . .

2 10½-oz. cans chicken
        broth
    Water
1 28-oz. can Italian tomatoes
    Reserved chicken pieces

Add chicken broth and water just to cover carrots; add tomatoes and top with chicken.

At this point you may stop and continue later.

Cooking ...

Over high heat, bring to boil; as soon as casserole steams, remove to preheated 350° oven and bake, covered, for 1 hour, or until chicken is tender.

Serve with ... French Bread (p. 120)
                    Watercress Salad (p. 132)

Chicken with Vegetables—V

French

A dish somewhat similar to Chicken with Vegetables—IV, but of less vigorous flavor.

You will need . . .

Preparation . . .

Assemble and prepare all ingredients.

6	**strips thick-sliced bacon, diced**
	Serving-pieces of chicken for 6 persons
	Salt
	Pepper

In casserole, render bacon until crisp; remove to absorbent paper and reserve. In remaining fat, brown chicken; season.

⅓ **cup cognac**

In saucepan, warm cognac, ignite it and pour over chicken; allow it to burn out. Remove chicken.

1 **onion, chopped**

In pan juices, cook onion until translucent.

3 **Tbs flour**
1 **bay leaf**
½ **tsp thyme**

To onion, add flour, bay leaf, and thyme and, over gentle heat, cook, stirring, for 5 minutes.

1½ **cups white wine**
1 **10-oz. can chicken broth**

To onion mixture, add liquids and, over high heat, cook, stirring, until sauce thickens. Replace chicken, spooning sauce over.

3 **Tbs butter**
12 **small white onions, peeled**
3 **medium potatoes, peeled and cut into ⅛'s**
3 **carrots, scraped and sliced**
3 **stalks celery, chopped**
½ **lb. mushrooms, sliced**

In skillet, heat butter and, in turn, glaze each vegetable, adding it to contents of casserole.

At this point you may stop and continue later.

Cooking . . .

Bake, covered, at 350° for 1 hour or until chicken and vegetables are tender.

Serve with . . . French Bread (p. 120)
Spinach Salad with watercress (p. 131)

Chicken with Vegetables—VI

Japanese

Delicate, light, and crunchy, a good spring-evening supper.

You will need ...

Preparation ...

Assemble and prepare all ingredients.

2   **Tbs butter**
2   **Tbs oil**
     Serving-pieces of chicken for 6 persons
     Salt
     Pepper

In casserole, heat butter and oil and brown chicken; season. Remove. Discard all remaining fat.

¼   **cup sherry**
2   **Tbs cornstarch**
1¾ **cups chicken broth**
2   **Tbs soy sauce**
½   **tsp ginger** *or* **1 Tbs preserved ginger, minced**
1   **tsp sugar**

Combine sherry and cornstarch, stirring until smooth. Add to broth; add seasonings. In casserole over high heat, cook liquid mixture, stirring, until sauce thickens. Replace chicken.

At this point you may stop and continue later.

Cooking ...

Bake, covered, at 350° for 1 hour, or until chicken is tender.

1   **can bamboo shoots**
3   **carrots, cut in 2" lengths very fine julienne**
¼   **lb. mushrooms, thinly sliced**
1   **9-oz. package frozen pea pods, thawed** *or*
1   **9-oz. package frozen French-style string beans, thawed**

Add vegetables and continue to cook, covered, at 350° for 15 minutes longer, or until vegetables are well heated but still crisp.

Serve with ... Rice (p. 115)

Chicken with White Wine

American

Quick, easy, and light, this dish was born of my desire for something care-free to cook on summer evenings.

You will need . . . 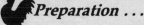 *Preparation . . .*

	Assemble and prepare all ingredients.
Seasoned flour Serving-pieces of chicken for 6 persons 2 Tbs butter 2 Tbs oil	In seasoned flour, dredge chicken. In casserole, heat butter and oil and brown chicken. Remove.
2 onions, chopped	In remaining fat, cook onion until translucent.
¼ tsp ground allspice ¼ tsp cinnamon ½ tsp ginger	To onion, add seasonings, stirring to blend mixture. Replace chicken. At this point you may stop and continue later. ## *Cooking . . .*
1¼ cups dry white wine 1 10-oz. can chicken broth	Combine liquids and pour over contents of casserole. Bake, covered, at 350° for 1 hour, or until chicken is tender.

Serve with . . . Noodles (p. 116)
                      Mixed Green Salad (p. 129)

Chicken with Yogurt

Indian

Very spicy and *very* good; the flavors are considerably stronger here than in the variation below.

You will need . . . 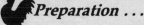 *Preparation . . .*

Assemble and prepare all ingredients.

continued . . .

2 cups yogurt
1 tsp cardamon, ground
½ tsp cumin, ground
1 tsp curry powder
½ tsp ginger
½ tsp dry mustard
½ tsp red pepper flakes
1 Tbs salt
½ tsp pepper
1 tsp sugar
1 clove garlic minced
¼ cup cider vinegar
  Juice ½ lemon

Serving-pieces of chicken
    for 6 persons

In container of blender, combine yogurt and seasonings; blend on low speed for 15 seconds.

In bowl, arrange chicken and pour yogurt mixture over; turn chicken to coat evenly. Marinate for 4 hours at room temperature; then marinate in refrigerator overnight.

At this point you may stop and continue later.

Cooking . . .

2 Tbs butter
2 Tbs oil

With rubber spatula, clean marinade from chicken, reserving the sauce. In casserole, heat butter and oil and brown chicken. Over browned chicken, pour marinade. Bake, covered, at 350° for 1 hour, or until chicken is tender.

Variation: Make marinade of 2 cups yogurt, 3 onions, chopped, 2 tsp cardamon, ½ tsp ginger, 1 Tbs turmeric, 1½ tsp salt, ½ tsp pepper. Proceed as above.

Serve with . . . Rice (p. 115)
    Mixed Green Salad (p. 129)

4. "...AND SOMETHING HEARTY TO GO WITH IT..."

Rice, Barley, and Bulgur

Rice, barley, and bulgur, among the most healthful and least fattening of the starches, are interchangeable in these menus. All three may be cooked in the same ways. All three lend themselves to various seasonings. All three give weight to a meal without making the eater feel heavy. All three are more easily prepared than noodles or spaghetti, for they absorb the liquid in which they are cooked, and thus require no last-minute draining.

There are two readily available kinds of rice at the supermarket. (Wild rice is not rice at all, but a member of the wheat family.) White or polished rice is the most used. Brown rice, free of its hull but unpolished, is the second variety. It takes longer to cook than white rice, but, I feel, has more body and taste and, if frozen, tends to hold up better. Of the white rices, there are long-grained, short-grained, Italian, Middle Eastern, and domestic varieties; each variety has its own characteristics, but all are cooked identically. I avoid precooked rice. I find natural rice more flavorful and of more pleasing consistency than precooked varieties. Preparing natural raw white rice requires at most only 25 minutes, and while the grain is actually cooking, you can do other things.

Barley comes in three sizes—small, medium, and large. I find that small barley does not give much "foundation" for a casserole sauce; large barley tends to become gummy when cooked (one reason why it is used to give body to soups). Medium pearl barley cooks up to both the right size and consistency.

Bulgur (also known as kasha, cracked wheat, or buckwheat groats) is a Middle Eastern food, popular also in Russia and the eastern European countries. It has a pleasant nutty flavor and, for freezing, performs perhaps best of the three grains.

A word about refrigerating and freezing rice, barley, and bulgur—both may be done successfully (I find the casserole method of cooking best). Before reheating to serve, however, the grain must reach room temperature. Reheating must be done over gentle heat. Heating cold cooked grains over high heat will result in an overcooked mush. Use a fork to stir the grain.

Basic recipe for boiled rice, barley, or bulgur: In
heavy saucepan with tight-fitting lid, heat 2 Tbs butter or oil. Add 1½ cups rice, barley, or bulgur, stirring with fork until each grain is coated. Add 3 cups water and 1 tsp salt; bring to the boil, stir once, reduce the heat, and simmer, covered, for 15 minutes, or until the grain is tender and liquid is absorbed. Allow about 25 minutes for barley and 45 minutes for brown rice.

Basic recipe for rice, barley, or bulgur en casserole:
In flame-proof casserole with tight-fitting lid, heat 2 Tbs butter or oil. Add 1½ cups rice, barley, or bulgur, stirring with fork until each grain is coated. Add 3 cups boiling water and 1 tsp salt, stir once, and bake, covered, at 350° for ...

18 to 25 minutes for white rice and bulgur
50 minutes for brown rice
45 minutes for barley

The flavor of rice, barley, and bulgur may be enhanced by seasonings. Before adding the water, season the grain with one or two of the following (suggested quantities are for 1½ cups grain, or 6 servings):

1 tsp ground allspice	1 tsp curry powder
½ tsp dried basil	½ tsp dried dillweed
1 bay leaf, broken	½ tsp dried marjoram
½ tsp dried chervil	

1   or 2 Tbs minced onion
   Grated rind ½ orange
¼   tsp dried rosemary, crum-
    bled

¼   tsp saffron, crumbled
½   tsp dried sage
½   tsp dried thyme
¾   tsp turmeric (for color)

In place of water, you may use: chicken broth or bouillon, beef broth or bouillon, consommé, home-made chicken or meat stock, clam juice, or orange juice.

The selection of cooking liquid will be determined by the principal flavoring of the accompanying chicken casserole.

To the cooked grain, you may add:

½   cup yogurt (typical Middle-
   Eastern treatment)
¼   cup currants or seedless
   raisins, plumped in
   boiling water and well
   drained
6   or 8 mushrooms, sliced and
   sautéed
2   or 3 Tbs minced parsley
2   or 3 Tbs pine nuts (*pignoli*)
2   or 3 Tbs toasted slivered almonds
3   scallions, finely chopped
   (with as much green
   as possible)
   Small jar pimentos,
   chopped.

The different flavors obtainable with rice, barley, and bulgur are virtually endless, dependent only upon your desire to experiment. If you remember that the quantity of liquid must be twice that of the grain, and that the liquid must be completely absorbed by the cooked grain, you will always have tender but well-shaped rice, barley, and bulgur. Any individuality you care to give the dish by use of liquid or seasonings will only enhance your meal; here is a challenging example of the creativity of cooking!

Noodles and Spaghetti

Noodles and spaghetti come in a bewildering variety of sizes and shapes. I prefer the thinner noodles and am especially fond of green noodles, which are made with spinach. Spaghetti #8, fettucini, vermicelli, and linguine are all excellent accompaniments to menus in this book.

To prepare: In a large saucepan or soup kettle, bring to boil 4 quarts (or more) salted water. Add the pasta of your choice. Immediately remove from the heat, stir once, and allow to stand, covered, for 20 minutes. At that time, drain, add soft butter, if desired, and serve. Cooking pasta by this method precludes sticking to the pan. If desired, 1 Tbs poppy seed may be added with the butter. For the most part, however, I find it unnecessary to add butter or any flavoring agent, preferring to use the noodles or spaghetti as a bed for the chicken dish. An 8-oz. box of noodles or a little more than half a 1-lb. box of spaghetti serves 6 persons adequately.

New Potatoes

French cooks know that one of the best accompaniments to dishes with sauce are boiled or steamed potatoes, served with butter and parsley, or served without embellishment to allow full enjoyment of the sauce. The trick with new potatoes is the timing: cooked too long, they turn to mush, cooked too short a time, their texture is uneven. Carefully prepared, they are a delight and should be highly considered in your menu-making.

To prepare: Scrub the small new potatoes well, but do not peel them (indeed, the red-skinned variety will give color interest to the meal). Put them in a large saucepan, add a generous sprinkling of salt, and cold water to cover. Bring to the boil and cook, covered, until just tender to the tines of a fork. About 15 minutes is sufficient for small new potatoes; about 20 minutes for somewhat larger ones. Drain and, if desired, peel the potatoes.

For steamed potatoes, prepare for cooking as suggested above. Put the potatoes in the perforated upper part of a vegetable steamer and, over rapidly boiling water, cook them, tightly covered, until tender (about 20 minutes for small new potatoes). Depending upon their size, 2 or 3 potatoes per person are ample.

Potato Pancakes

German

I have always enjoyed potato pancakes when I did not have to make them! This method obviates all hard work—and therefore I heartily endorse it.

To prepare: In blender, combine 2 eggs, 1 tsp salt, 3 Tbs flour, 2 onions, coarsely chopped, and 5 medium potatoes, peeled and coarsely chopped. Cover and blend on high speed. Add 1 potato, peeled and coarsely chopped and 1 tsp baking powder; blend very briefly. Drop 1 Tbs batter onto well-buttered hot griddle. Cook until golden on the bottom; turn and cook other side.

Potato mixture will turn gray if prepared in advance of cooking, but with this speedy method, the entire operation can be a last-minute and unharried operation.

Hominy

American

Hominy, which derives its name from an Algonquian word meaning to grind corn, is whole or ground hulled corn from which the bran and germ have been removed by processing the whole kernels in a lye bath.

Whole hominy comes in three can sizes, 16, 20 and 29 ounces. Two 20-oz. cans serve 6 persons. *To prepare:* empty the contents of the can into a saucepan and heat, covered, until of desired temperature. Strain, add 2 Tbs soft butter, and toss. If desired, 1 Tbs poppy seed may be added with the butter.

Hominy grits, or ground hominy, is found on the cereal shelf of the supermarket. *To prepare:* there are two methods. 1) In a saucepan, bring 5 cups water to boiling, add 1 tsp salt, and 1 cup hominy grits; cook, covered, stirring often, for 25 to 30 minutes. 2) In a double boiler, combine 4 cups boiling water, 1 tsp salt, and 1 cup hominy grits; cook, covered, over briskly boiling water for 45 minutes. Add 2 Tbs soft butter, and stir until cereal is blended.

Breads

Few foods are more appealing to the eater or more fun to make than breadstuffs. The scent of freshly baked bread is one of my cherished boyhood memories. Making bread is not difficult. The dough itself needs time to rise, but the number of minutes which the cook must spend actively creating the breadstuff are few indeed when compared to the pleasure derived from baking and eating homemade bread.

There follows a basic recipe for homemade bread, together with five variations. Directions are also given for corn meal muffins, cream biscuits, and, for those who want to make their own accompaniment for cheese, I include a recipe for *pita*, Middle Eastern flatbread.

Homemade Bread—Basic Recipe

The pleasure of this recipe lies in its ease of preparation and versatility (see the variations below).

You will need . . .	*Preparation . . .*
	Assemble all ingredients.
2 **packets dry yeast** 2 **cups warm water** *or* **milk** 3 **Tbs butter, melted** 2 **Tbs sugar** 2 **tsp salt**	In warm bowl, dissolve yeast in liquid; add next three ingredients, stirring to dissolve sugar and salt.
4 **to 4½ cups unbleached** **flour**	Add flour, 1 cup at a time, mixing until smooth; dough will be soft and sticky.
	Cover bowl with cloth and put in a warm place; let dough rise until doubled in bulk. Stir down.
	Spoon into 2 buttered 8x4½-inch loaf pans, 2 1-quart casseroles, or muffin tins.
	Cover and let dough rise until doubled in bulk.
	Bake at 375° for about 50 minutes, or until loaves sound hollow when tapped. (Rolls baked in muffin tins will require only 15 to 20 minutes.) Remove from pans and cool on rack.

Variations:

1) *Cardamon bread or rolls* (a Swedish favorite): Use milk; to liquid ingredients, add 2 beaten eggs, 1 Tbs ground cardamon seed, and ½ cup seedless raisins.

2) *French bread* (In France, bread contains no shortening and stales rapidly; therefore it is most frequently baked and eaten the same day.

This recipe yields a bread near the consistency of French loaves. I have found it impossible, however, to reproduce exactly the taste or "feel" of native French bread—one of the glories of France!): Follow basic recipe, using 1½ cups water and 1 Tbs sugar; use 1 cup whole wheat flour and 2¾ cups unbleached white flour. On floured surface, knead well; allow to rise until doubled in bulk, punch down, knead again, and allow to rise until doubled in bulk; punch down, knead, form into 2 loaves and place them on baking sheet sprinkled with corn meal; allow to rise again, brush with melted butter, and, with sharp knife, make 3 or 4 diagonal slashes across top of loaves; bake at 400° for 30 minutes; allow to cool on rack before brushing off excess cornmeal.

3) *Herb-flavored bread or rolls:* To dry ingredients, add 1 Tbs dillweed or oregano or rubbed sage or thyme.

4) *Rolls* (A recipe from the south, handed down by Grandmother Boucher—see Chicken with Dumplings. You will find these rolls *very* rich and very light.): Use milk, substitute lard for butter; increase sugar to ½ cup; to liquid ingredients, add 2 beaten eggs.

5) *Wholewheat bread or rolls:* Substitute 2 cups wholewheat flour for 2 cups of the 4 to 4½ cups unbleached flour.

Corn Meal Muffins

The following recipe for corn meal muffins, far simpler than the traditional one requiring separating the eggs, comes from the Pennsylvania Amish country.

You will need . . .   *Preparation . . .*

Assemble all ingredients.

1	cup flour	In mixing bowl, sift together dry ingredients.
1	cup corn meal	
4	tsp baking powder	
½	tsp salt	
2	Tbs sugar	

1	egg, beaten	Combine egg, milk, and butter; add to dry ingredients, and stir only enough to blend together.
1	cup milk	
3	Tbs melted butter	

Drop batter into well greased, hot muffin tins, filling each ⅔ full. Bake at 425° for 20 to 25 minutes. Yield: 12 muffins.

Variations:

For richer muffins, omit milk; combine 1 cup sour cream with ¼ cup milk, and use as liquid ingredient with egg and shortening.

Add, with liquid ingredients, 2 Tbs chopped pimento, 1 Tbs chopped onion.

Add 2 Tbs finely chopped parsley.

Add ⅓ cup grated Parmesan cheese.

Cream Biscuits

This recipe yields a rich biscuit. If desired, light cream may be used for a less caloric one!

continued . . .

You will need ...	Preparation ...
	Assemble all ingredients.
1½ cups flour 1 Tbs baking powder 1 tsp salt	Mix thoroughly dry ingredients.
1 cup heavy cream Grated rind of 1 lemon *or* of 1 orange	Combine liquid ingredients. Combine dry and liquid ingredients, stirring to moisten flour. Drop dough from spoon onto well-buttered cookie sheet or into muffin pans; bake at 400° for about 10 minutes, or until golden. Yield: between 12 and 18 biscuits.

Pita (Flatbread)

Middle Eastern

My most helpful encounter with Middle Eastern cuisine and hospitality has been in Boston, no less! I have never understood how a busy designer finds so much time and energy for cooking and entertaining, but Joseph Shakra not only delights his own friends with this culinary skill but is almost a catering service to all who share his enthusiasm for food. From him comes this recipe for *pita* to accompany Middle Eastern main dishes, to complement *hommos* and *baba ghanouge,* and to set off fine cheese.

You will need ...	Preparation ...
	Assemble all ingredients.
1 tsp sugar ½ tsp salt ¾ cup hot water 1 packet dry yeast	In mixing bowl, combine sugar, salt, and hot water; stir to dissolve sugar and salt. Allow to cool to lukewarm. Sprinkle yeast over and allow to dissolve.
2 cups flour	Add flour, ½ cup at a time. Turn dough onto floured surface and knead thoroughly. Divide dough into 12 small pieces. Roll dough pieces into balls. With rolling pin, roll each ball as thinly as possible and place on cookie sheet. Bake the rounds at 500° for about 7 minutes, or until puffed and golden.

5. "…A BIG, CRISP SALAD…"

While it is true that salad-tossing should be a last-minute operation, done just before serving, the preparation of the salad greens and other ingredients and of the dressing may be undertaken ahead of time. What a boon the plastic bag is to the cook who would like to enjoy family or guests or both! Greens and vegetables for salads may be readied and stored in the refrigerator. Salad greens may be kept together. Their accompaniments (onion, cucumber, etc.) should be kept separately so that each component of the salad will retain its own special flavor.

The following salad greens go well together in almost every combination:

Chinese or celery cabbage
endive
escarole
lettuce (all kinds)

rugola (or arugola or roquette or
    rocket)
spinach
watercress

One or more of the following vegetables may be added to the greens:

artichoke hearts
avocado pear (peeled at the
    time of serving, otherwise
    it will darken)
canned bamboo shoots
raw broccoli stalk, peeled and
    cut in julienne strips
cherry tomatoes, whole or
    halved
cucumber, sliced
green pepper, in julienne strips
raw sliced mushrooms (sprin-
    kling them with lemon
    juice will prevent their
    darkening)

radishes, sliced
red onion rings
scallions (I prefer them sliced
    lengthwise in 2-inch strips)
sweet red pepper, in julienne
    strips
canned water chestnuts, sliced

Bacon bits are particularly flavorful in salad. Three strips, diced, rendered until crisp, and drained on absorbent paper, will give a pleasant lift to salad for 6 persons.

If fresh herbs are available to you, nothing will give salad more interest than the addition of one or two of the following, cut fine with scissors:

basil (both sweet and opal)
chervil
chive
dillweed

marjoram
oregano
parsley
tarragon

The dried herb will also enhance salad; do not hesitate to use it. It is difficult to say how much, for the quantity used is a matter of personal taste.

You may further embellish your salad with croutons or mimosa egg (hard-boiled egg put through a sieve).

Salad Dressings

1. *A dependable "all-purpose" dressing:* In a jar with tight-fitting lid, combine 2 tsp sugar, 1 tsp salt, ½ tsp white pepper, ½ tsp dry mustard (optional) and ¼ cup lemon juice or vinegar of your choice; shake until sugar and salt are dissolved. Add ¾ cup oil of your choice; shake until well blended.

2. *A highly-seasoned dressing to store for long periods:* In a quart jar with tight-fitting lid, combine 1 cup red wine vinegar, ½ cup semi-dry sherry, ½ cup French vermouth, ¼ cup red wine, 1 tsp each: dry mustard, seasoned salt, pepper, monosodium glutamate, 2 tsp sugar, and 4 cloves garlic, peeled and crushed. Shake well and let stand at room temperature for several hours; store in refrigerator. When using, combine 1 part this mixture with 3 or 4 parts oil of your choice.

3. *A dressing especially good for spinach salads:* In blender, combine 1 clove garlic, 1 tsp sugar, grated rind and juice of 1 lemon, ½ tsp salt, ¼ tsp paprika, ¼ tsp pepper, 4 Tbs sour cream, and ½ cup olive oil. Blend at low speed for 15 seconds.

4. *A slightly sweet dressing, good on mild-flavored greens:* In a jar with tight-fitting lid, combine ¼ cup mild honey, ¼ cup olive oil, juice of 1 lemon, a dash of aromatic bitters, ¼ tsp salt, and ¼ tsp white pepper. Shake until thoroughly blended. (If desired, a sliver of garlic may be marinated in dressing 1 hour and removed.)

5. *A dressing especially good for romaine:* In blender, combine 2 cups sour cream, 4 tsp tarragon vinegar, 1 onion, chopped, ½ tsp celery salt, ½ tsp each: sweet basil, oregano, thyme, ½ tsp salt, ¼ tsp white pepper, 1 clove garlic, chopped. Blend at low speed for 15 seconds.

6. *A refreshing dressing for calorie-watchers:* In blender, combine 1 cup buttermilk, 2 Tbs sour cream, ¼ tsp dry mustard, ½ tsp Worchestershire sauce, ¼ tsp white pepper, 1 tsp powdered cumin, 1 tsp dillweed, ½ clove garlic (optional). Blend at low speed for 15 seconds.

Artichokes

This method of preparing artichokes comes from Jean Westbrook, who entered my life at the seashore where she was ever busy at the many duties of a "Kindly Harbor Mistress"—counting the sanderlings, taking census of the quahog clams in the Great South Bay, and testing for ripeness the crop of beach plums. A violinist-turned-author, Jean has acted as secretary to several of the world's great operatic ladies, including Miss Pons and Miss Steber. Her accounts of these experiences lead one to wonder who was the greater diva—employer or employee.

To prepare: Allowing one medium artichoke per serving, remove stems and rinse them under cold water. In a soup kettle, combine 1 tsp salt, 8 peppercorns, 1 tsp sugar, 1 clove garlic, split, ½ tsp oregano *or* thyme, and ½ tsp red pepper flakes. Add artichokes, bottoms down, and cold water to cover half of artichokes. Bring to boil and cook, covered, for 20 to 25 minutes. Drain and rinse under cold water; allow to cool. If desired, serve chilled; I feel the vegetable has more flavor if eaten at room temperature. Serve with dressing #1.

Beans in Garlic Oil

This unusual salad tastes like the Middle East. I do not know its origin, but find that it goes nicely with Middle-Eastern menus. Serve it as a side dish to the chicken casserole of your choice.

To prepare: In colander, rinse under cold water 1 20-oz. can red kidney beans and 1 20-oz. can white beans or *canelloni.* Drain thoroughly. Into ⅓ cup olive oil, press 2 cloves garlic; add juice of 1 lemon, ½ tsp pepper, ½ tsp salt. Shake to blend well. In serving bowl, put beans, pour dressing over, add ½ cup chopped parsley and 1 small red onion, chopped; toss gently until well mixed. Allow to marinate for 2 hours before serving. (If desired, fresh basil may be substituted for the parsley.)

Cucumber Salad

Cucumber salad goes particularly well in summer weather, when the cool taste and crisp texture of this vegetable are at their best. (Botanically, cucumber is a fruit.)

To prepare: Pare the cucumbers (often cucumbers have been waxed to preserve them). Slice them thin, dice them, or cut them in strips; if you

use either of the latter two treatments, quarter the cucumbers first and remove the seeds with a spoon. If desired or necessary, cucumbers may be crisped by soaking in cold salted water for about one-half hour—no longer. The cucumber may be served on lettuce or alone with any of the oil-base dressings given here; cream or sweet dressings rob the vegetable of its taste.

Green Salad with White Grapes

So attractive to look at, so cool to taste. The sweet grapes make the salad seem very like a dessert. Excellent after almost any of the casseroles, and particularly welcome after highly spiced ones.

To prepare: Make a selection of salad greens (I enjoy Boston lettuce, romaine, and a bit of rugola); prepare them as for Mixed Green Salad (p. 129). Arrange the greens in a salad bowl and add ½ lb. seedless grapes, rinsed (if desired, grapes may be cut in lengthwise halves).

Toss with dressing #1, #2, #5, or #6.

Garnish the salad with red onion rings.

Green Bean Salad

Green beans, when in season, are inexpensive and healthful—and never more flavorful than when eaten cold.

To prepare: Pick over 1½ lbs. green beans and rinse them in cold water. In large saucepan or soup kettle, bring to boil 4 quarts water, seasoned with 1 Tbs salt and 1 Tbs sugar; add 1 tsp soda. Add the beans and, when water returns to boiling, cook, uncovered, for about 12 minutes, or until beans are just tender. At once remove from heat, drain, and, under cold water, cool the beans. Allow to drain thoroughly; chill.

The beans should be tender but still crunchy; and the soda should have turned them a rich dark green.

Toss the beans with dressing #1, #2, #4, or #5.

Garnish the salad with halved cherry tomatoes, red onion rings, and/or sliced mushrooms.

Lentils with Oil and Lemon

An unusual salad which goes well with Greek and Middle-Eastern menus.

To prepare: Following directions on package, cook 2 cups lentils, seasoned with 1 onion stuck with 3 cloves, 1 bay leaf crumbled, and ½ tsp salt. It is important not to overcook the lentils. Drain well, discard onion and bay leaf. Allow to cool. In serving bowl, gently toss lentils with 6 scallions, chopped (with as much green as possible) and ½ cup chopped parsley. Combine the juice of 1 lemon, ⅓ cup olive oil, 1 tsp sugar, ½ tsp salt, and ¼ tsp pepper. Blend well and pour over lentils, tossing gently until lentils are evenly coated. Refrigerate before serving.

Mixed Green Salad

The most familiar of all tossed salads has no rule of thumb for its preparation; its success depends in large measure, I feel, upon experimenting with different combinations—all work well, but you will find favorites of your own.

To prepare: Select a combination of salad greens which appeals to you (such as iceberg and Boston lettuce with spinach; or celery cabbage with watercress; or romaine and Boston lettuce—the combinations are endless). Rinse the greens well, drain, and shake off excess water (swinging them in a large muslin towel is a good way). Put the greens in a large salad bowl and, with scissors, cut them through in several directions until of uniform bite size. (Yes, I admit that to cut salad greens is heresy, but the technique works without bruising tender leaves.)

To the greens may be added:

> cherry tomatoes
> *or*
> sliced tomato
> ¼ lb. mushrooms, rinsed,
>   dried on absorbent
>   paper, and sliced
> 6 scallions
> *or*
> red onion rings

Sometimes I use all three—plus bacon bits and croutons. The menus given in this book make the salad a full course unto itself, not merely a side dish.

At the time of serving, toss the salad with dressing #1, #2, #4 (depending upon your choice of salad ingredients), #5, or #6.

Mushrooms with Herbs

A piquant salad which, if desired, may be simmered in its marinade for 5 minutes and served hot.

To prepare: In container with tight-fitting lid, combine ½ cup olive oil, 1 clove garlic, put through a press, 1 Tbs each: chopped chives, grated onion, chopped parsley; ¼ tsp each: pepper, tarragon, thyme; ¾ tsp salt, ½ tsp sugar, and 3 Tbs lemon juice. Shake well to blend and pour over 1 lb. mushrooms, rinsed, dried on absorbent paper, and sliced; toss gently to coat well. Allow to marinate for at least 2 hours.

"Oriental" Salad

The name is in quotation marks only because the salad is made up of vegetables used in oriental cuisine.

To prepare: Select a combination of vegetables from:

> Chinese or celery cabbage
> spinach
> watercress

Select a combination of accents from:

> canned bamboo shoots

cucumber	radishes
green pepper	scallions
mushrooms	water chestnuts

To whatever combination you prefer, add 1 9-oz. package frozen pea pods, cooked as per directions on the box (do *not* overcook) and chilled.

Toss together all ingredients with dressing #1 or #4. If desired, sprinkle over shreds of grated raw beet or carrot.

Spinach Salad

Colorful, tasty, and crisp, spinach salads are delightful endings to the meal.

To prepare: In cold water, rinse thoroughly a 10-oz. packet of spinach (for a more bountiful salad, use 2 packets, or add another green to the 10-oz. one); remove the woody stems and fibrous veins in the leaves by pulling them toward the tip of the leaf. Shake or pat dry with absorbent paper.

In salad bowl, arrange spinach and add your choice of:
¼ lb. mushrooms, rinsed, dried
      on absorbent paper, and
      sliced

sweet red pepper, cut in ju-
    lienne strips
water chestnuts, sliced
watercress
or
any other salad accent

Spinach salad is made especially festive by the addition of 3 navel
oranges, peeled, sectioned, and seeded. Add a sprinkling of tarragon.

Toss with dressing #1, #3, #4, #5, or #6.

Watercress Salad

One of the most spirited salad greens, watercress is very good following
bland-sauced casseroles. It will keep for two or three days, refrigerated
with its stems well immersed in water. A large bunch serves 6 adequately, but 2 bunches are better if you use salad as a vegetable.

To prepare: Cut or break off larger woody stems from the watercress
branches. Rinse them well in cold water, drain them, and shake dry.
(Swinging them in a large muslin towel is a fine way to remove excess
water.) When ready to serve, arrange watercress in salad bowl and toss
with dressing #1, #3, or #6.

To add red onion rings, peel and slice thinly a small red onion, separate
the circles and toss over the salad after it has been dressed. If desired,
the red onion may be coarsely chopped, but it is less decorative this
way. (If small or medium red onion is not available, use what you need
of a large one; the remainder will keep for several days plastic-wrapped
in the refrigerator.)

To add parsley, cut the parsley leaves from the stem; unless they are
very large, leave them whole. About ½ cup leaves will improve any
salad.

6. "...WITH CHEESE..."

This listing makes no pretense of being complete; the choices are largely personal, reflecting what I have enjoyed and have found to go well with the dishes in this book. The identification by nationality will enable the cook to offer a regional cheese, if desired. Individual entries, briefly describing the cheeses, are alphabetically arranged.

It is impossible to verbalize tastes and flavors. The taste of cheese is no exception. Indeed, cheeses are particularly difficult to describe because of their subtlety and bouquet, because of their flavor seeming to change in combination with other food and drink, and because of their aftertaste. For these reasons, to whet the reader's appetite, I have tried to suggest the quality of the flavor rather than attempt a definition of the taste itself—a foolhardy and, indeed, impossible undertaking.

To savor fully the taste of cheese, serve it with a bland wafer, not with a cracker or bisquit tasty in its own right. A trip to a cheese shop and a few questions to the proprietor will help here; there are many wafers, flatbreads, and crackers made expressly to accompany and flatter the taste of cheese. Try some of these. Or try *pita* (p. 123).

Most of these cheeses go well with salad. Some of them, however, are special—both in flavor and texture—so that you will want to serve them after salad, with an additional glass of wine, as a fitting end to the meal. In these cases, a suggestion to this effect is made.

Countries of origin:

American

Baronet
Cheddar
Farmer Cheese
Liederkranz
Muenster
Neufchâtel
Sage
"Swiss"

Austrian

Liptauer

Danish

Blue
Crema Dania

Dutch

Edam
Gouda

English

Caerphilly
Cheddar
Cheshire

Gloucester
Stilton

French

Bonbel
Boursault
Boursin
Brie
Camembert
Caprice des Dieux
Chèvre
Coulommiers
Gourmandise
Pont l'Évêque
Port-Salut
Reblochon
Roquefort
St. Paulin

German

Bierkäse

Greek

Feta

Italian	**Swedish**
Bel Paese	Hablé Crème Chantilly
Fontina	
Gorgonzola	**Swiss**
Ricotta	
	Emmenthal
	Gruyère

The cheeses individually:

Baronet (American)—A mild, buttery cheese, this is reminiscent of both Bel Paese and Muenster. It goes well with salads containing onion or scallions. Available in supermarkets.

Bel Paese (Italian)—Of delicate flavor, this increasingly popular cheese is imported and also made domestically in Wisconsin. Of creamy texture, it has a pleasant hint of tartness. An excellent all-purpose table cheese, it complements any salad. Available at supermarkets.

Bierkäse (German)—"Beer cheese" is strong and goes well with hearty meals. Made domestically in Wisconsin, in a version less strong than the imported German. Available at supermarkets (domestic) and cheese shops (imported).

Blue (Danish)—The "Scandanavian Roquefort" is of smoother consistency than its French counterpart, which tends to crumble. Of strong, rich flavor, Danish Blue is the most reasonably priced of imported blue-veined cheeses. Available at supermarkets.

Bonbel (French)—This bland cheese, the size of a small Edam, is creamy and tastes somewhat like Muenster, but perhaps milder. It goes well with any "uncomplicated" salad. Available at supermarkets (usually) and cheese shops.

Boursault (French)—Boursault and Boursin, very rich triple-crème cheeses, are elegant additions to any meal. Both are expensive. They should be served as a course by themselves, following salad. Available at cheese shops.

Boursin (French)—See Boursault. Boursin has added flavorings.

Brie (French)—This is one of the best and most popular of French cheeses. It should have the same degree of ripeness throughout—often

difficult to find—and, when the crust is gently pressed, the center should bulge but not run. Available at supermarkets (domestic) and cheese shops (imported).

Caerphilly (English)—A white, firm cheese related to Cheddar, Caerphilly from Wales tastes somewhat like buttermilk—*real* buttermilk, that is, not cultured. It has a slightly salty tang and, while a short-lived cheese, can be kept for some time in a damp cloth. Available at cheese shops.

Camembert (French)—"Invented" in 1790 by a farmer's wife in the village of Camembert, this celebrated cheese is now made throughout France. A statue has been erected to the good Mme. Harel, and with reason, for this perhaps best known of cheeses has a pleasing creaminess and a flavor somewhat similar to Brie, but milder and smoother. Camembert does not travel well and, when bought cut from its wheel, should be eaten soon. Available at cheese shops. Domestic and other "adaptations" are available at supermarkets, but I advise buying the real thing.

Caprice Des Dieux (French)—A delicious, mild, and costly *fondant* which deserves to be served as dessert to crown the meal. Available at cheese shops.

Cheddar (American)—New York and Wisconsin Cheddars usually have a full-bodied, sharp flavor, although mild Cheddars are on the market. While perhaps not an elegant accompaniment to salad, Cheddar is always a satisfying table cheese. Available at supermarkets.

Cheddar (English)—There are two kinds of Cheddar in England, homemade and factory-made. The homemade cheese is not exported and the factory-made, while excellent, is not, I feel, sufficiently different (or, indeed, better) than our domestic Cheddar to warrant the increased price. Available at cheese shops.

Cheshire (English)—A superb cheese, it does not keep very well (it may be stored for a normal length of time wrapped in a damp cloth). Cheshire has a pleasant salty flavor which derives from the grazing lands where it is made. A recommended accompaniment to salads. Available at cheese shops.

Chèvre (French, a good deal of the time)—*Chèvre* is a generic name for cheeses made with goat's milk, and while many do come from France,

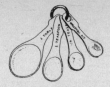

they are also made throughout Europe. Of the many different kinds of *Chèvre,* perhaps the most popular in this country is Valençay. Frequently goat cheese is available cut from a large loaf. The taste is that of strong cream cheese; the consistency is usually drier. Available at cheese shops.

Coulommiers (French)—This is soft cream cheese made in the Brie country. Usually eaten in France (that is, without leaving home), it is processed for export. Its flavor is mild—a buttery Camembert. Available at cheese shops.

Crema Dania (Danish)—Neither a Scandinavian Brie nor Camembert, this cheese has its own taste, reminiscent perhaps of its French cousins, but distinctive and perhaps more delicate. It ripens evenly, is reasonably expensive, and deserves its own place on the menu. Available at supermarkets and cheese shops.

Edam (Dutch)—A cheese of light, buttery flavor and firm but moist texture, historically Edam is one of the oldest cheeses still eaten (Holland exported it during the Middle Ages). It keeps well and is satisfying for persons newly experimenting with the delights of cheese. Available at supermarkets and cheese shops.

Emmenthal (Swiss)—Named for the place of its origin, the Emme Valley in Bern Canton, Emmenthal, together with Gruyère, is the most celebrated Swiss cheese. Called in this country merely "Swiss cheese," it should have a nutty flavor and a sweetish aftertaste. In Switzerland, these qualities are attributed to the particular grazing material eaten by the cattle and to the glacial water which they drink. Available at supermarkets and cheese shops.

Farmer Cheese (American)—A first cousin to cottage and pot cheese, Farmer Cheese has a mild and slightly sour taste. It is a good hot-weather cheese, keeping well and tasting cool in summer. Available at supermarkets.

Feta (Greek)—A "pickled" cheese of sheep's milk; that is, it has been put down in a mixture of milk, salt, and water. The flavor is somewhat sharp and pungent, an excellent accompaniment to any meal of Middle Eastern orientation. Available at supermarkets (canned) and cheese shops (bulk).

Fontina (Italian)—One of the superior Italian cheeses, this buttery delight is made in large wheels, looks rather like Emmenthal, and tastes like Gruyère flavored with a little Brie. It keeps well and should be served with pride at any meal of Italian origin. Available at supermarkets (sometimes) and cheese shops.

Gloucester (English)—Originally made from the unusually rich milk of the Gloucester cow, now all but extinct, Gloucester cheese has a pungent taste and firm texture. "Double" Gloucester is exported to this country, the "single" never is. Even so, Gloucester is not always readily found; if you come upon some, buy it! Available at cheese shops.

Gorgonzola (Italian)—The celebrated blue-veined cheese from Italy deserves place with France's Roquefort and England's Stilton. It travels well and for this reason one is fairly sure of its quality. The softest of the blue-veined cheeses, it does not crumble. Its flavor, recalling Roquefort, is robust but smooth. Available at supermarkets (domestic) and cheese shops (imported, which in this case, is *far* superior).

Gouda (Dutch)—Smooth and mellow, with a flavor similar to that of Edam, Gouda is made from whole milk (Edam is not), and is therefore creamier in texture. Ordinarily only young Goudas are exported to this country; but an aged one, worth your search, has a considerably fuller taste. Available at supermarkets and cheese shops.

Gourmandise (French)—This "dessert" cheese has a very creamy texture, smooth and buttery. In France, it is flavored with kirsch; that made for export is flavored with cherry extract. No matter, with its rich sweetness, it is a satisfying end to any French meal. Available at cheese shops.

Gruyère (Swiss)—As much a part of Switzerland as the Alps or yodeling, Gruyère resembles Emmenthal in appearance and taste, but is actually more delicate and is the preferred of the two when a Swiss diner makes his choice. The Gruyère made in this country, individually foil-wrapped in triangular shapes, has nothing to do with the original Swiss product; it is rubbery, tasteless, and without character—insist on the real Gruyère. Available at supermarkets (sometimes) and cheese shops.

Hablé Crème Chantilly (Swedish)—Despite its name, this is a Scandinavian cheese which recalls the fabulous Frommage Monsieur of France, rarely found in this country. Fortunately, Hablé is purchasable here and is, like Gourmandise, a fine ending to the meal. Available at supermarkets (sometimes) and cheese shops.

Liederkranz (American)—Yes, despite both its name and strong flavor, Liederkranz is an American cheese, first developed at Monroe, New York, in 1882. It should be eaten at room temperature (as, indeed, should all cheeses) and fully ripened. When the cheese is thoroughly soft, it has the texture of heavy honey. Unlike many soft-ripening cheeses, Liederkranz is not only dependable, but also far more delicate to the palate than to the nose. Highly recommended. Available at supermarkets.

Liptauer (Austrian)—A favorite in the Austria-Hungary-Bulgaria section of Europe, Liptauer is a "made" cheese—the mixing of a bland cheese with butter and seasonings. It serves well as accompaniment to salad; it is also good as a cocktail spread. My recipe for Liptauer comes from Ljuba Welitsch, the former Metropolitan Opera soprano, who also contributed Chicken with Sour Cream.
Ingredients should be at room temperature. Through a sieve, force ½ pint cottage cheese; blend it well with 1 3-oz. package cream cheese and 4 Tbs butter. Add 1 tsp anchovy paste, 1 onion, grated, 1½ tsp paprika, ½ tsp salt, and ¼ tsp white pepper. Mix thoroughly and refrigerate overnight in plastic or crockery container with close-fitting lid. Recipe may be doubled, if desired.

Muenster (American)—First developed in Alsace, Muenster or Munster was next made in France and, finally, produced—and very well—in this country. European Muenster is a soft cheese, strong-tasting and rather smelly. American Muenster is more bland, smoother, and an excellent accompaniment to salads. The cheese sold in bulk is much superior to the packaged variety. Available at supermarkets (packaged) and cheese shops (bulk).

Neufchâtel (American)—Like cream cheese in taste, color, and texture, Neufchâtel contains less butterfat and more protein. Richer than the French Neufchâtel, from which it derives, the American cheese is much easier to procure. Available at supermarkets.

Pont L'Évêque (French)—Semi-hard fermented cheese made from whole or skimmed milk, Pont l'Évêque is one of France's most important cheeses. Its taste is considerably milder than its scent. When at its best, plump and soft to the touch, it is an admirable "meal-ender," and almost the perfect complement to red wine. Available at cheese shops.

Port-Salut (French)—A creamy, yellow, whole-milk cheese, Port-Salut

first came from the Trappist Monastery near Port du Salut, but is now made, after a secret formula, in Trappist monasteries the world over. Port-Salut is a buttery cheese, similar in texture to Bel Paese, but with a considerably stronger taste. In France, Port-Salut, Port-du-Salut, and St. Paulin are virtually the same cheese. There is Danish as well as American Port-Salut. Available at supermarkets and cheese shops.

Reblochon (French)—This soft cheese from Savoy is made of ewe's milk. Reblochon is pale-cream colored; its crust is reddish. If old, it tends to turn bitter, but when *à point* (the peak of ripeness), it has a distinctive and delicious flavor. Available at cheese shops.

Ricotta (Italian)—Creamy, bland, and slightly sweet, Ricotta is the cottage cheese of Italy, but smoother and without curds. It is made from the coagulable substance in whey, derived, in turn, from the manufacture of other cheese. In this country, Ricotta is made from a combination of whey and whole milk. Sprinkled with sugar, it can be eaten as a sort of dessert pudding. Available at supermarkets.

Roquefort (French)—Originally from a little town bearing its name in Aveyron, Roquefort is the most celebrated of the blue-veined cheeses. Roquefort continues to be produced in this district and it is especially good with red Bordeaux wine and should follow salad rather than be eaten with it. Available at supermarkets (sometimes) and cheese shops.

Sage (American)—Sage cheese is really a bland, white Cheddar flavored with oil of sage. "Vermont Sage," as it is generally called, actually has no sage in it; nevertheless, it is a good, tasty cheese with salads. Available (seasonally) at supermarkets and cheese shops.

St. Paulin (French)—See Port-Salut.

Stilton (English)—"English Roquefort," made from whole milk with added cream, does not defer to its Continental cousin. Praised by Alexander Pope, Jane Austen, and Charles Lamb, Stilton tastes like a combination of blue-veined cheese and Cheddar. It is mellow and crumbly.

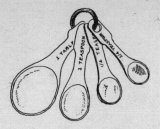

It does not keep very long or very well, and should be wrapped in a moist cloth. Highly recommended. Available at cheese shops.

"Swiss Cheese" (American)—See Emmenthal.

Two Middle Eastern Spreads

In Middle Eastern countries, *hommos* (chick-pea puree) and *baba ghanouge* (eggplant puree) are often eaten on *pita* (flatbread) in place of cheese. For the cook who would enjoy offering such regional fare, there follow recipes for both *hommos* and *baba ghanouge*.

Hommos

Middle Eastern

In a blender, combine 1 20-oz. can of chick-peas, drained (reserve the liquid), ⅓ cup lemon juice, and 2 cloves garlic, peeled. Blend until the mixture is smooth. If necessary, add a *little* liquid from the can. To the contents of the container, add ⅓ cup *tahineh* and blend until the mixture is homogenous; if necessary, add a little sesame seed or olive oil to aid blending. (*Tahineh* is sesame seed puree, available at Greek, Middle Eastern, and health-food stores.)

Baba Ghanouge

Middle Eastern

With a fork, prick a large eggplant several times; on a cookie sheet, bake it at 400° for 1 hour, or until soft. Cool. Skin the eggplant and put the pulp into a blender. To the eggplant, add 5 Tbs *tahineh* (see recipe above), 1 tsp salt, ½ tsp pepper, the grated rind and juice of 1 lemon, and ¾ tsp prepared horseradish (optional); blend at low speed until mixture is homogenous. Chill before serving.

7. "...AND THEN FRUIT!"

As suggested in the section, "To Plan Your Meal . . ." only a bit of forethought is needed to enable you to serve ripe fresh fruit for dessert. A mid-February visit to my local supermarket revealed three varieties of apples, two kinds of pears, grapefruit, pineapple, oranges, tangerines, plums, and two kinds of melon.

On the canned fruit shelf, I found grapefruit, oranges, mandarin oranges, pears, peaches, cherries, apricots, pineapple, prunes, and plums. These singly or in combination may be given added interest by folding them into sour or whipped cream, by steeping them in wine, or by adding a bit of spice.

Among the frozen fruits, I found rhubarb, strawberries, raspberries, blackberries, melon balls, cherries, peaches, and pineapple. Fully thawed and drained, frozen fruit may be treated in any of the ways suitable for canned fruits.

Thus, from the three categories of fruit available, even during "off season," it is possible to offer a tasty, light, and healthful dessert. Fruit desserts may be as simple as a single shiny red apple or as complicated as a fresh fruit cup, or *macedoine* (a fruit cup with kirch or other liqueur added). As added suggestions, there follow recipes for dried-fruit compote, fruit pudding, and fruits in red wine.

Dried-Fruit Compote

Always welcome when fresh fruit is unavailable, dried-fruit compote is "international" (I know of no country which does not have it in some form) and therefore may be used in a regional menu or in one selected at random from among dishes which simply appeal to you.

To prepare: In a baking dish with tight-fitting lid, combine 1 box dried mixed fruit, 1 cup seedless raisins, 3 cups water, ⅓ cup brown sugar, packed, the rinds and juice of 1 lemon and 1 orange, a 3" piece of stick cinnamon, and pinch of salt. Bake, covered, at 325° for 1 hour; allow to cool, remove rinds, and chill. If desired, serve with whipped cream or a dollop of sour cream.

The compote may be also made with only one variety of dried fruit: apricots, peaches, pears, or prunes.

Fruit Pudding
French

In France, this dish would be made with *crème fraîche,* natural heavy cream wherein the lactic acids and natural ferments have worked until the cream has thickened and taken on a nutty flavor. *Crème fraîche* is delicious, but for some reason unavailable in this country. Well-drained canned fruits (apricots, peaches, pears) may be substituted for fresh fruit; so, too, may frozen fruits, thawed and well drained. If desired, the dish may be served with either table or whipped cream; I prefer it plain and at room temperature, not directly from the refrigerator.

To prepare: In a mixing bowl, blend well 3 Tbs sugar and 2 tsp flour; add 2 cups commercial sour cream, 2 tsp vanilla extract (or almond, lemon, or orange), and 2 eggs. Beat well. In a baking dish, arrange peach halves from ripe fruit, peeled and pitted (or pear halves from ripe fruit, peeled and cored). Pour over sour cream mixture and bake, uncovered, at 350° for 30 minutes. Remove from oven, allow to cool, and chill in refrigerator. Sprinkle pudding with extra-fine granulated sugar and place under very hot broiler to carmelize (about 5 minutes—no more). Allow to cool and return to refrigerator.

If desired, a topping may be used in place of the carmelized sugar: mix together ¼ cup flour, ¼ cup brown sugar, packed, ½ tsp nutmeg, and 2 Tbs soft butter. Mixture should resemble crumbs. Sprinkle over pudding after first 15 minutes of cooking and continue baking another 15 minutes.

Fruit in Red Wine

Another way of treating ripe peaches or pears or canned fruits is to steep them in red wine:

To prepare: In a saucepan, combine ⅔ cup red wine, ⅔ cup orange juice, ½ cup sugar, 8 whole cloves, a 3" piece of stick cinnamon, and the peel of 1 lemon; bring to boiling point, reduce the heat, and simmer, covered, for 15 minutes. Over peach or pear halves, peeled and pitted or cored, arranged in a serving bowl, pour the hot wine mixture; cover and allow to cool before chilling in refrigerator.

If canned fruits are used, in place of the orange juice use ⅔ cup syrup in which the fruits are packed; omit sugar altogether.

8. APPENDIX

Roast Chicken

A 4½ or 5½-pound chicken will serve six persons. It is sometimes more convenient, however, to use two 2½- or 3-pound chickens; in this way, there is more breast meat, more second joints, and often the roasted fowl is more moist. If you are limited for time, two smaller chickens will roast more quickly than will a single, larger bird.

Tie or skewer the legs of the cleaned fowl, which should be at room temperature before cooking, and place, breast side up, on a greased rack in a roasting pan. Place the pan in a preheated 450° oven; reduce the heat to 350°. Allow 20 minutes per pound for an unstuffed bird; slightly less time per pound is adequate for stuffed fowl. For moist, tender roast chicken, it is important not to overcook. The chicken will carve more easily if allowed to stand about 15 minutes after cooking. Serve the roast fowl with one of the following sauces:

Pan Gravy: Add 1 cup water to roasting pan, scraping and stirring to deglaze it; over moderate heat, cook for a few minutes and season to taste with salt and pepper. If desired, dry white wine may be substituted for water.

Thickened Gravy: To pan juices, add 2 Tbs flour, stirring to blend mixture; add 1 cup warm water and, over moderate heat, cook, stirring, until sauce thickens.

Giblet Gravy: Proceed as for Thickened Gravy (above); add giblets, cooked in cold water to cover, seasoned with ½ tsp salt, and minced; use giblet water as liquid ingredient of the gravy.

Stuffing: Stuffing is not obligatory, but does make a nice addition to roast fowl; and it is a good menu substitute for potato or other starchy food. Stuff the fowl just before cooking it. Handle stuffing lightly, otherwise it will be heavy and sodden. Do not pack stuffing, but allow room for it to expand while cooking; this will assure its lightness. Extra stuffing may be cooked in a buttered baking dish and served separately from the chicken. Allow approximately 1 cup of stuffing per 1 pound of fowl.

Once the fowl is stuffed, truss it: skewer the cavity and, with a long string, lace, back and forth, on the outside of the skewers (*see illustration*). Then, tightening the string as you would a shoe lace, wrap the ends around the lower ends of the legs and around the tail; pull the string tight and tie it (*see illustration*). Skewer or tie the wings to the body; draw the neck skin over the back and secure it with a skewer. (On left-hand illustration, skewers are drawn out-size for demonstration purposes.)

Stuffing may be made easily and tastily from commercially prepared bread crumbs, croutons, or packaged seasoned bread dressing, all readily available at the supermarket.

For those who wish to prepare their own breadstuff for stuffing: use bread several days old and dry it thoroughly in a 250° oven, until crisp but not brown. A food chopper or electric blender are two means of reducing the bread to crumbs. I prefer the old fashion way of putting the bread in a bag (a muslin bag is best, for it will not tear—the danger in using a paper one); use a rolling pin to crush the bread in the bag.

For lighter, dryer stuffing, the bread may be cut in small cubes and lightly browned in a 250° oven (this is the method I most often use).

Basic Stuffing:
Using forks, toss together 4 cups breadstuff, 1 stick butter, melted, ½ tsp salt, ¼ tsp pepper, and 1 onion, minced. Any further addition or embellishment expresses your culinary inventiveness. To activate such creative impulse, herewith follows a variety of stuffings.

(Note: if you use Basic Stuffing alone, increase breadstuff to 5 cups. In the fruit stuffings, suggested below, a combination of fruits is possible, and in almost any proportion—apple, apricot, cranberry, orange, pineapple, prune, or raisin.)

Apple Stuffing:
In 4 Tbs butter, cook for 5 minutes ½ cup celery (with leaves), chopped, 1 onion, chopped, and 2 Tbs fresh parsley, chopped. Add 4 cups tart apple, peeled and diced, ¼ cup brown sugar, packed, ½ tsp salt, and ¼ tsp each marjoram, sage, and thyme. Cook, stirring, for 5 minutes. Toss together apple mixture with 2 cups Basic Stuffing. (If desired, the proportions of apple and breadstuff may be reversed. Also, the sugar may be omitted in place of ¾ cup seedless raisins, plumped for 5 minutes in boiling water. A clove of garlic, chopped and cooked with the onion, makes a nice flavor accent.)

Apple-Apricot-Orange Stuffing:
In 4 Tbs butter, cook 2 onions, chopped, until translucent. Combine ½ cup celery leaves, chopped, 2 large apples, peeled and diced, 15 tenderized dried apricots, chopped, the grated rind of 1 orange, 1 cup diced orange meat, and ½ tsp each ginger and marjoram; stir to blend mixture. Toss together onion and fruit mixture with 1 8-oz. package prepared stuffing. If necessary, moisten the stuffing with a little Madeira wine.

Apricot Stuffing:
Toss together 1½ cups tenderized dried apricots, chopped, and Basic Stuffing. If desired, the stuffing may be moistened with apricot juice. (The addition of ½ cup celery, chopped, gives a nice taste variation.)

Bulgur Stuffing: See Rice Stuffing (p. 149).

Celery Stuffing: In 2 Tbs butter, cook for 5 minutes 1 cup celery, chopped, 1 onion, chopped, and 4 Tbs fresh parsley, chopped. Toss together celery mixture and ½ tsp each celery seed and poultry seasoning with Basic Stuffing. If desired, moisten lightly with water.

Corn Stuffing: Toss together 1 cup whole kernel canned corn, drained, and 1 8-oz. package of cornbread stuffing, prepared according to directions given on the package.

Cranberry-Pineapple Stuffing: In 4 Tbs butter, cook ½ cup celery, chopped. In blender, coarsely chop 1½ cups cranberries, washed and drained. Toss together celery, cranberries, ⅓ cup sugar, 1½ cups drained pineapple tidbits, and ½ tsp nutmeg with Basic Stuffing. If desired, moisten slightly with reserved pineapple juice.

Cucumber Stuffing: In ¼ cup water, cook for 15 minutes giblets and 1 cup celery, chopped. Cool and reserve broth. Chop giblets, discarding leathery parts of gizzard. Toss together celery, giblets, 1 onion, chopped, 1½ cups cucumber, peeled and diced, and ½ tsp sage with Basic Stuffing. If desired, moisten with a little of reserved broth.

Fruit Stuffing: Toss together 1½ cups mixed fruit cocktail, well drained, and ½ tsp thyme with Basic Stuffing. If desired, ½ cup pecans, chopped, may be added.

Giblet Stuffing—I: In cold, slightly salted water to cover, simmer giblets for 15 minutes. Cool and reserve broth. Chop giblets, discarding leathery parts of gizzard. Toss together giblets with Basic Stuffing. Use reserved broth to moisten the dressing.

Giblet Stuffing—II: In 4 Tbs butter, cook for 5 minutes ½ lb. mushrooms, sliced, and 1 onion, chopped. In ¼ cup Madeira wine, cook giblets, covered, for 15 minutes. Cool and reserve broth. Chop giblets, discarding leathery parts of gizzard. Toss together mushroom mixture, giblets, ¼ cup celery, chopped, 3 Tbs fresh parsley, chopped, and ¾ tsp tarragon with Basic Stuffing. Moisten the dressing with reserved broth.

Herb Stuffing: Sweet basil, marjoram, summer savory, and thyme are pleasant additions to stuffing. Use 1 tsp each, if dried; 1 Tbs each, chopped, if fresh. Toss together with Basic Stuffing.

Mint Stuffing: In 4 Tbs butter, cook for 5 minutes 1 onion, chopped, and 1 stalk celery, chopped. Add ¾ cup fresh mint leaves, chopped. Toss together mint mixture with Basic Stuffing.

Mushroom Stuffing: In 4 Tbs butter, cook for 5 minutes ½ lb. mushrooms, washed, drained, and coarsely chopped. Toss together mushrooms with Basic Stuffing.

Onion Stuffing: In boiling, slightly salted water, cook 6 onions for 10 minutes. Drain well and chop. Toss together with Basic Stuffing.

Orange Stuffing: In 4 Tbs butter, cook 1 cup celery, chopped, and 1 onion, chopped, for 5 minutes. Peel 2 large navel oranges; dice the orange meats, removing membranes and reserving juice. Toss together onion mixture, orange meat, the grated rind of 1 orange, and ¾ tsp poultry seasoning with Basic Stuffing. Moisten the dressing with about ¼ cup reserved orange juice.

Oyster Stuffing: Cook gently 1 pint oysters until edges just begin to curl. Drain and reserve liquor. If oysters are small, use whole; if large, quarter them. Toss together oysters and ½ tsp mace with Basic Stuffing. Moisten the dressing with about ¼ cup reserved oyster liquor mixed with the juice of ½ lemon.

Parsley Stuffing: Toss together ¾ cup finely chopped fresh parsley with Basic Stuffing.

Prune Stuffing: See Apricot Stuffing (p. 147), substituting pitted tenderized prunes for apricots.

Rice Stuffing: In skillet, render 6 slices bacon, diced. Remove to absorbent paper and reserve. Discard all but 2 Tbs fat. In fat, cook 1 onion, chopped, until translucent. Toss together bacon bits, onion, 1 cup celery, chopped, 4 cups cooked rice (or bulgur), ½ tsp salt, ¼ tsp pepper, and ½ tsp nutmeg with 1 cup breadstuff. Moisten with ¼ cup water.

Sausage Stuffing: Render until brown and crisp ½ lb. sausage meat. Remove to absorbent paper and drain well. Toss together sausage, 3 Tbs fresh parsley, chopped, and ½ tsp nutmeg with Basic Stuffing.

Chicken Livers

Chicken Livers with Bacon Sauce: In heavy skillet, cook
6 pieces thick-sliced bacon, diced, until crisp and golden; remove to
absorbent paper and reserve. Discard all but 3 Tbs fat. In fat, cook 1½
lbs. chicken livers, halved, for 4 minutes, 2 minutes per side. Remove
and reserve. In fat, cook 3 onions, coarsely chopped, and 3 green peppers, seeded and coarsely chopped, until onion is translucent. Add 1
generous Tbs flour, 1 tsp paprika, ½ tsp thyme, ½ tsp salt, and ¼ tsp
pepper; stir well to blend mixture. Add 1 10-oz. can chicken broth,
stirring over high heat until sauce thickens. Simmer, covered, for 15
minutes. To sauce, add reserved chicken livers. Serve over hot, buttered
noodles and top with reserved bacon bits.

Chicken Liver Pudding: From 1 lb. chicken livers, remove
membranes and fat; soak in cold salted water to cover for 1 hour. Drain
on absorbent paper. In a blender, combine livers, 1 cup light cream, 2
eggs, 2 Tbs potato starch, ½ tsp salt, and ½ tsp nutmeg; cover and blend
on low speed for about 30 seconds, or until mixture is smooth. While
blender is running, add ¼ cup milk, ¼ cup sherry, and, if blender is
sufficiently large, 1 cup light cream. Pour mixture into a buttered 1- or
1½-quart mold and set in a pan filled with 1" hot water. Bake at 325°
for 1 hour, or until pudding is set and a sharp knife inserted at center
comes out clean.

Sauce for Chicken Liver Pudding: Mix together 1 cup
sour cream, 1 generous Tbs dillweed and 2 tsp prepared horseradish.
(The longer the sauce has to work, the better it tastes.) On a warm plate,
unmold the pudding, and, if desired, sprinkle with dillweed or chopped
fresh parsley. Serve the sauce separately.

If desired, the livers may be forced through a sieve rather than
pureed in the blender; also, the additions of milk, sherry, and second
cup of cream may be made in a mixing bowl—essential if the blender
does not hold 5½ cups.

Chicken Livers in Ramekins (a delicacy from the south-
ern United States): From 1 lb. chicken livers, remove membranes and
fat; soak in cold salted water to cover for 1 hour. Drain on absorbent
paper. In a blender, combine livers, 3 eggs, 3 Tbs heavy cream, 1 Tbs
melted butter, ¼ tsp salt, a dash of pepper, and 2 Tbs fresh parsley,
chopped; cover and blend on low speed for about 30 seconds, or until
mixture is smooth. Add 6 mushrooms, washed and drained, and blend
for 5 seconds. Pour liver mixture into 6 buttered ramekin molds; set the
molds in a shallow pan and add hot water to within ¼" of top of

ramekins. Bake at 350° for 20 minutes, or until custard is set and a sharp knife inserted at center comes out clean. The custard may be unmolded or eaten from the individual dish with a spoon.

If desired, the livers may be forced through a sieve rather than pureed in the blender.

Chicken Livers with Rice: In seasoned flour, dredge 1½ lbs. chicken livers. In casserole, heat 6 Tbs butter and brown livers quickly, about 3 minutes per side. Remove and reserve. In remaining butter, cook 2 onions, chopped, until translucent. Add 1½ cups raw natural rice, stirring to coat well with butter. Add 2 Tbs fresh parsley, chopped, ½ tsp sweet basil, 1 tsp salt, and ¼ tsp pepper. Pour over 3 cups chicken broth, boiling. Bake, covered, at 350° for about twenty minutes; arrange reserved livers on top of rice and continue to cook, covered, for 10 minutes, or until livers are thoroughly heated and the rice is tender and the liquid absorbed.

Chicken Livers Sautéed with Wine: In seasoned flour, dredge 1½ lbs. chicken livers. In heavy skillet, heat 4 Tbs butter and brown livers rapidly, about 3 minutes per side. Add ½ cup cognac or madeira or marsala or sherry or dry red or white wine (igniting, if cognac) and, over moderate heat, cook until the liquid boils gently and the sauce is slightly thickened. Garnish with chopped fresh parsley.

Chicken Liver Soufflé: From 1 lb. chicken livers, remove membranes and fat; soak in cold salted water to cover for 1 hour. Drain on absorbent paper. In a blender, reduce livers to a liquid consistency; if desired, livers may be pressed through a sieve. In saucepan, melt 4 Tbs butter; add 5 Tbs flour, stirring, and cook gently for a few minutes. Add 1 cup milk and cook, stirring, until mixture thickens. Add ½ tsp salt, ¼ tsp pepper, ½ tsp nutmeg, and pureed chicken livers; remove from heat. Add 4 egg yolks, beaten until light, and stir until mixture is thoroughly blended. Beat 5 egg whites and ½ tsp cream of tartar until stiff; fold into liver mixture. Pour into an unbuttered soufflé dish set in a pan of hot water and bake at 325° for about 45 minutes.

Chicken Livers—Sweet and Sour: In saucepan, combine 2 Tbs sugar, 1 tsp salt, 3 Tbs soy sauce, 6 Tbs cider vinegar, juice from 1 20-oz. can pineapple chunks, and 1 tsp ginger. In casserole or heavy skillet, heat 4 Tbs butter and brown 1½ lbs. chicken livers quickly, about 3 minutes per side. Remove and reserve. In remaining butter, cook for a few minutes, stirring, 1 green pepper, coarsely chopped, 1 cup mushrooms, sliced, 1 Tbs preserved ginger root, 1 can water chestnuts, quartered, and reserved pineapple chunks. Combine 2 Tbs cornstarch and ¼ cup water, stirring to blend well; add to pineapple juice mixture

and, over high heat, cook until sauce thickens. Pour sauce over contents of casserole and top with reserved livers. Serve with rice.

Chicken Livers with Tomato Sauce: In seasoned flour, dredge 1½ lbs. chicken livers. In casserole, heat 6 Tbs butter and brown livers quickly, about 3 minutes per side. Remove and reserve. In remaining butter, cook 2 onions, chopped, until translucent. Add ¾ tsp salt and ¼ tsp pepper. Add ¼ lb. mushrooms, sliced, and 2 whole canned tomatoes, drained, *or* 2 ripe fresh tomatoes, skinned, seeded, and chopped. Cook until mushrooms are tender, about 5 minutes. Add ½ tsp dried basil (or 1 generous tsp fresh chopped basil) and 1½ cups heavy cream; cook, stirring, until the mixture thickens (do not allow it to boil). Add reserved chicken livers, spooning the sauce over. Cook only long enough to heat livers thoroughly. Serve over rice or noodles.

Dumplings

In making dumplings, *always* combine *separately* dry and liquid ingredients. Put them together only at the time of cooking and mix them only enough to moisten the dry ingredients; the dough should be lumpy. Drop the dough by the spoonful onto the simmering contents of the casserole. Dumplings require about 20 minutes to cook, covered; do not remove casserole cover after dumpling dough has been added. If you wish to use dumplings as accompaniment to various of the casserole recipes in this book (and dumplings go well with many of them), add the dumpling dough only for the final 20 minutes of cooking the chicken casserole.

Basic Dumplings: In one bowl, combine 1 cup flour, 2 tsp baking powder, and ½ tsp salt. In another bowl, combine 1 beaten egg, ⅓ cup milk, and 2 Tbs shortening (vegetable oil or melted butter). Combine and mix only until flour is moistened; proceed as in the paragraph above. Makes 6 dumplings. To double recipe: use ¾ cup milk, 1 egg, and double all other ingredients; to cook doubled recipe, the pan must be wide.

Cheese Dumplings: To dry ingredients, add ¼ cup grated Parmesan cheese.

Cornmeal Dumplings: Use 1/3 cup flour. Add milk to ½ cup fine cornmeal and let stand 30 minutes; add egg to milk-meal mixture. Combine with dry ingredients. Especially good with casseroles with tomato-based sauces.

Parsley Dumplings: To dry ingredients, add ¼ cup fresh parsley, minced.

Poppy Seed Dumplings: To dry ingredients, add 1½ tsp poppy seed.

Savory Dumplings: To dry ingredients, add ½ tsp poultry seasoning, ½ tsp celery seed *or* marjoram *or* thyme, and 1 tsp minced onion.

Spinach Dumplings: To dry ingredients, add spinach, washed, dried, and chopped to equal 1 cup.

Watercress Dumplings: To dry ingredients, add watercress, washed, dried, and chopped to equal ¼ cup.

Whole-Wheat Dumplings: Use 2/3 cup white flour combined with ⅓ cup whole-wheat or graham flour.

INDEX

A

Apples, chicken with, 10
Artichoke hearts, chicken with, 12
Artichokes, 127
"Assemble and prepare all ingredients," explained, 3
"At this point you may stop and continue later," explained, 3
Avocado, chicken with, 14

B

Baba ghanouge, 141
Bacon, use of, 8
Bacon sauce
  chicken livers with, 150
  chicken with, 15
Bananas, chicken with, 16
Barley
  basic recipes for, 115
  description of, 114
  seasonings for, 115
Baronet cheese, 135
Bean salad, green, 128
Beans and sausage, chicken with, 18
Beans in garlic oil, 127
Beef, chicken with, 19
Beer, chicken with, 20
Bel Paese cheese, 135
Bierkäse cheese, 135
Bing cherries, chicken with, 21
Biscuits, cream, 122

Blue cheese, 135
Bonbel cheese, 135
Bouillon cubes (or powder), chicken, 4
Bourbon whiskey, chicken with, 22
Boursault cheese, 135
Boursin cheese, 135
Bread, 119
  cardamon, 120
  French, 120
  herb-flavored, 121
  homemade, 120
  pita, 123
  white, 120
  whole-wheat, 121
Brie cheese, 135
Broth, chicken
  preparation of, 4
  use of, 4
"Brown chicken; season," explained, 3
Brown rice, chicken with, 23
Bulgur (bulghur)
  basic recipes for, 115
  chicken with, 24
  description of, 114
  seasonings for, 115
Butter (and margarine), use of, 4, 7

C

Cabbage, red, chicken with, 79
Cabbage, white, chicken with, 25